15
Canadian
Poets

15 Canadian Poets

Edited by GARY GEDDES
and PHYLLIS BRUCE

Toronto
Oxford University Press
1970

Except where otherwise indicated
all the photographs are by
SHELDON GRIMSON

SBN 0-19-540177-8

7 8 9 10 11 — 0 9 8 7 6

Printed & bound in Canada by
THE BRYANT PRESS LIMITED

CONTENTS

PREFACE

It would be impossible to write a critical preface to this anthology without repeating much of what is written in the notes, so we have decided to spare the reader the task of wading through quotations and generalizations that he will encounter later in more meaningful contexts. We have tried in our selections to suggest the unusual scope and variety of poetry written in English in Canada since the Second World War; at the same time, we wanted to provide a selection in depth from the work of each poet. We decided, finally, to limit the number of poets to fifteen so that we could include mature, established writers (Birney, Layton, Souster, Avison, Purdy), writers in the middle of their poetic careers (Nowlan, Cohen, Jones, and Mandel), and young writers (Atwood, Newlove, Bowering, MacEwen, Coleman, and Ondaatje). Some of the poets were easier to represent in a short space than others; it was necessary to give extra space to one or two poets in order to include poems, especially longer poems, that seemed indispensable. Ultimately there are no prescriptive criteria to offer for choices that are highly subjective; it can only be hoped that the book reflects what is happening in the art itself.

The poets appear according to the date of their first published collection; and their poems, as far as it was possible to ascertain, in the order in which they were written. The notes on each poet, which are rather long and impressionistic, are printed alphabetically for easy reference.

We are grateful to the poets for their co-operation in providing the correct texts for poems and in the very personal matter of being photographed. Also, we would like to acknowledge the untiring assistance and encouragement of William Toye of the

Oxford University Press. Finally, we would like to express our appreciation to Sheldon Grimson for his sensitive photographs, which provide an added dimension to the book.

Toronto   GG
October 1970   PB

ACKNOWLEDGEMENTS

MARGARET ATWOOD 'Some Objects of Wood and Stone' and 'The Islands' reprinted from *The Circle Game* by Margaret Atwood by permission of Miss Atwood and The House of Anansi.

Reprinted by permission of Oxford University Press (Canadian Branch): 'The Animals in That Country', 'A Night in the Royal Ontario Museum', and 'Progressive Insanities of a Pioneer' from *The Animals in That Country* by Margaret Atwood; 'Further Arrivals', 'Death of a Young Son by Drowning', and 'The Immigrants' from *The Journals of Susanna Moodie* by Margaret Atwood; 'Game After Supper', 'Procedures for Underground', and 'Younger Sister, Going Swimming' from *Procedures for Underground* by Margaret Atwood.

MARGARET AVISON 'Snow', 'The World Still Needs', 'New Year's Poem', 'To Professor X, Year Y', 'The Swimmer's Moment', 'Voluptuaries and Others', and 'Birth Day' reprinted from *Winter Sun* by Margaret Avison by permission of Miss Avison.

'Pace', 'Black-White Under Green: May 18, 1965', 'July Man', 'The Absorbed', 'In a Season of Unemployment', and 'A Nameless One' reprinted from *The Dumbfounding*, poems by Margaret Avison, by permission of W.W. Norton & Company, Inc. Copyright © 1966 by Margaret Avison.

EARLE BIRNEY All poems reprinted by permission of Dr Birney and The Canadian Publishers, McClelland and Stewart Limited, Toronto: 'November Walk Near False Creek Mouth' from *Selected Poems 1940-1966* by Earle Birney; the remaining poems from *The Poems of Earle Birney*.

GEORGE BOWERING Reprinted by permission of Mr Bowering: 'The Night Before Morning' and 'Grandfather' from *Points on the Grid* by George Bowering; 'To Cleave', 'The Swing', and 'Esta Muy Caliente' from *The Man in Yellow Boots* by George Bowering; 'News' and 'Circus Maximus' from *The Silver Wire* by George Bowering (published by The Quarry Press).

'Indian Summer' and 'Albertasaurus' reprinted from *Rocky Mountain Foot* by George Bowering by permission of The Canadian Publishers, McClelland and Stewart Limited, Toronto.

'The House', 'The Egg', 'Dobbin', and 'Our Triple Birth' reprinted from *The Gangs of Kosmos* by George Bowering by permission of Mr Bowering and The House of Anansi.

LEONARD COHEN   All poems reprinted from *Selected Poems, 1956-1968* by Leonard Cohen by permission of The Canadian Publishers, McClelland and Stewart Limited, Toronto.

'God Is Alive' reprinted from *Beautiful Losers* by Leonard Cohen by permission of The Canadian Publishers, McClelland and Stewart Limited, Toronto.

VICTOR COLEMAN   All poems reprinted by permission of Mr Coleman: 'The Lady Vanishes' and 'Kenkyusha: Day Nine' from *one/eye/love* by Victor Coleman; 'The Devil' and 'Fish : Stone : Song' from *Light Verse* by Victor Coleman; 'Parking Lots for Greg Curnoe' is uncollected.

D. G. JONES   'Portrait of Anne Hébert', 'Little Night Journey', 'Odysseus', 'Beautiful Creatures Brief as These', 'For Françoise Adnet', and 'These Trees Are No Forest of Mourners' reprinted from *The Sun is Axeman* by D.G. Jones by permission of University of Toronto Press. Copyright, Canada, 1961 by University of Toronto Press.

'Summer Is a Poem by Ovid', 'I Thought There Were Limits', 'On a Picture of Your House', 'Beyond the Photograph', 'Nocturne: In the Way of a Love Song', and 'The Stream Exposed With All Its Stones' reprinted from *Phrases from Orpheus* by D.G. Jones by permission of Oxford University Press (Canadian Branch).

IRVING LAYTON   All poems reprinted by permission of The Canadian Publishers, McClelland and Stewart Limited, Toronto: 'If I Lie Still' from *Balls for a One-Armed Juggler* by Irving Layton; 'Marché Municipale' from *The Shattered Plinths* by Irving Layton; the remaining poems from *Collected Poems* by Irving Layton.

GWENDOLYN MACEWEN   'Poems in Braille', 'You Cannot Do This', 'Green With Sleep', 'Manzini: Escape Artist', and 'Arcanum One' reprinted from *A Breakfast for Barbarians* by Gwendolyn MacEwen by permission of The Ryerson Press, Toronto.

'The Red Bird You Wait For', 'The Discovery', 'Inside the Great Pyramid', 'One Arab Flute', and 'Dark Pines Under Water' reprinted from *The Shadow-Maker* by Gwendolyn MacEwen by permission of The Macmillan Company of Canada Limited.

'Memoirs of a Mad Cook', which first appeared in *The Canadian Forum*, is reprinted by permission of Miss MacEwen.

ELI MANDEL   Reprinted by permission of Mr Mandel: 'A Castle and Two Inhabitants', 'Acis', and 'Pillar of Fire' from *Fuseli Poems* by Eli Mandel; 'The Meaning of the I CHING', 'Houdini', 'Pictures in an Institution', 'Woodbine', 'The Speaking Earth', 'From the North Saskatchewan', and 'Marina' from *An Idiot Joy* by Eli Mandel; 'On the 25th Anniversary of the Liberation of Auschwitz', which first appeared in *The Canadian Forum*.

'Thief Hanging in Baptist Halls' reprinted from *Black and Secret Man* by Eli Mandel by permission of The Ryerson Press, Toronto.

JOHN NEWLOVE   Reprinted by permission of Mr Newlove: 'The Arrival' from *Elephants, Mothers & Others* by John Newlove; 'Then, If I Cease Desiring', 'The Flowers', and 'Verigin, Moving in Alone', from *Moving in Alone* by John Newlove.
Reprinted by permission of The Canadian Publishers, McClelland and Stewart Limited, Toronto: 'Crazy Riel', 'Everyone', 'Lady, Lady', 'Ride Off Any Horizon', and 'In This Reed' from *Black Night Window* by John New-love; 'The Engine and the Sea', 'Warm Wind', and 'The Flower' from *The Cave* by John Newlove.

ALDEN NOWLAN   'Beginning' and 'Warren Pryor' reprinted from *Under the Ice* by Alden Nowlan by permission of The Ryerson Press, Toronto.
'God Sour the Milk of the Knacking Wench' and 'For Nicholas of All the Russias' reprinted from *Wind in a Rocky Country* by Alden Nowlan by permission of Mr Nowlan.
Reprinted by permission of Clarke, Irwin & Company Limited: 'I, Icarus', 'And He Wept Aloud, So That the Egyptians Heard It', 'Britain Street', 'In Those Old Wars', and 'July 15' from *Bread, Wine and Salt* by Alden Now-lan; 'The Mysterious Naked Man', 'Another Parting', 'For Claudine Be-cause I Love Her', 'Ypres: 1915', and 'The First Stirring of the Beasts' from *the mysterious naked man* by Alden Nowlan.

MICHAEL ONDAATJE   All poems reprinted by permission of Mr On-daatje: 'We're at the Graveyard' first appeared in *Quarry* and ' "The gate in his head" ' in *Ant's Forefoot*; 'Postcard from Picadilly' is uncollected; the remaining poems are from *The Dainty Monsters* by Michael Ondaatje.

AL PURDY   Reprinted by permission of The Canadian Publishers, McClel-land and Stewart Limited, Toronto: 'The Cariboo Horses', 'Song of the Impermanent Husband', and 'Transient' from *The Cariboo Horses* by Al Purdy; 'Eskimo Graveyard' and 'Arctic Rhododendrons' from *North of Summer* by Al Purdy; 'Detail', 'Interruption', 'Lament for the Dorsets', and 'The Runners' from *Wild Grape Wine* by Al Purdy.
'The Beavers of Renfrew', which first appeared in *The Canadian Forum*, is reprinted by permission of Mr Purdy.

RAYMOND SOUSTER   'The Nest' reprinted by permission of Mr Souster.
Reprinted by permission of The Ryerson Press, Toronto: 'Young Girls', 'Lagoons, Hanlan's Point', 'The Lilac Poem', 'Downtown Corner News Stand', 'Study: The Bath', 'Flight of the Roller-Coaster', 'The Six-Quart Basket', and 'The Death of the Grenadiers' from *The Colour of the Times* by Raymond Souster; 'A Morning in Brussels', 'Memory of Bathurst Street', and 'St Catherine Street East' from *Ten Elephants on Yonge Street* by Raymond Souster.

'All This Slow Afternoon' and 'The Embarrassment' reprinted from *Lost and Found* by Raymond Souster by permission of Clarke, Irwin & Company Limited.

'On the Rouge', 'Night Raider', and 'Among the Willows' reprinted from *As Is* by Raymond Souster by permission of the Oxford University Press (Canadian Branch).

'The First Two Acorns' and 'Get the Poem Outdoors' reprinted from *So Far So Good* by Raymond Souster by permission of Oberon Press.

Birney - 70's
B.C
-depression
-poet, novelist
- wide range of topics
-Socialist
- university circuit
- Grand Ola man of Canadian Poetry
- B.C oriented

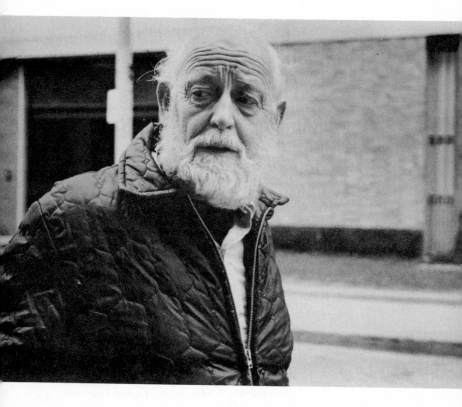

Earle Birney

From the Hazel Bough

I met a lady
   on a lazy street
hazel eyes
   and little plush feet

her legs swam by
   like lovely trout
eyes were trees
   where boys leant out

hands in the dark and
   a river side
round breasts rising
   with the fingers' tide

she was plump as a finch
   and live as a salmon
gay as silk and
   proud as a Brahmin

[Handwritten annotations:]

- ambiguous, shifting, images
- lady on street - prostitute
- brief encounter
- no trees, bright, cheerful, short, ties no hard feelings
- little feet, pretty, lively, gay, young, proud, lots of laughs
- wonders where she is going who she is with, what is doing now
- concrete objects with abstract ideas - objective correlatives - girl & objects he associates with her.
- hazel, grow wild, bear hazel nuts
- half green half brown material - plush, silk, soft
- trout - legs
- lovely eyes, thinks about boys
- no man sees where her legs are now.

technique? Lang?

1

we winked when we met
   and laughed when we parted
never took time
   to be brokenhearted

but no man sees
   where the trout lie now
or what leans out
   from the hazel bough

[Handwritten margin notes: carefully constructed stanzas / no capitals / Brahim – upper-class / India / – salmon, Hazel – BC]

Bushed

[Handwritten above title: Bushed – alone, sanity, too long, treeless / area of arctic, cabin fever.]

He invented a rainbow but lightning struck it
shattered it into the lake-lap of a mountain
so big his mind slowed when he looked at it

[Handwritten: goes out to bush, leaves city / going back to nature, natural / Great Can Dream]

Yet he built a shack on the shore
learned to roast porcupine belly and
wore the quills on his hatband

[Handwritten: – built shack on shore / – dominated by mts. / – 1st stanza dream – / back to nature garden of eden.]

At first he was out with the dawn
whether it yellowed bright as wood-columbine
or was only a fuzzed moth in a flannel of storm
But he found the mountain was clearly alive
sent messages whizzing down every hot morning
boomed proclamations at noon and spread out
a white guard of goat
before falling asleep on its feet at sundown

[Handwritten: – shack trapping / – caught local / animals de then / – got up early full of energy / – mts. begin to work / – vibrations]

When he tried his eyes on the lake ospreys
would fall like valkyries
choosing the cut-throat
He took then to waiting
till the night smoke rose from the boil of the sunset

[Handwritten: – goats – sent them down to keep out / Garrison mentality / stay in day – go out night • night / no butter owls bears moose]

[Handwritten bottom: – winds – most frightening thing mt peaks / – paranoia – shacked up.]

[Handwritten left margin: Conceived better than Achieved]

But the moon carved unknown totems
out of the lakeshore
owls in the beardusky woods derided him
moosehorned cedars circled his swamps and tossed
their antlers up to the stars
Then he knew   though the mountain slept   the winds
were shaping its peak to an arrowhead
poised

And now he could only
bar himself in and wait
for the great flint to come singing into his heart

1951

A Walk in Kyoto

All week   the maid tells me   bowing
her doll's body at my mat   is Boys' Day
Also please Man's Day   and gravely
bends deeper   The magnolia sprig in my alcove
is it male?   The ancient discretions of Zen were not shaped
for my phallic western eye   There is so much discretion
in this small bowed body of an empire
the wild hair of waterfalls combed straight
in the ricefields   the inn-maid retreating
with the face of a shut flower   I stand hunched
and clueless like a castaway in the shoals of my room

When I slide my parchment door to stalk awkward
through Lilliput gardens framed and untouchable
as watercolors   the streets look much the same
the Men are being pulled past on the strings of their engines
the legs of the Boys are revolved by a thousand pedals
and all the faces as taut and unfestive as Moscow's
or Chicago's   or mine

Lord Buddha help us all there is vigor enough
in these islands and in all islands reefed and resounding
with cities   But the pitch is high as the ping
of cicadas   those small strained motors concealed
in the propped pines by the dying river   and only
male as the stretched falsetto of actors mincing
the women's roles in *kabuki*   or female only
as the lost heroes womanized in the Ladies' Opera
Where in these alleys jammed with competing waves
of signs in two tongues and three scripts
can the simple song of a man be heard?

By the shoguns' palace   the Important Cultural Property
stripped for tiptoeing schoolgirls   I stare at the staring
penned carp that flail on each other's backs
to the shrunk pool's edge for the crumb this non-fish
tossed   Is this the Day's one parable?
Or under that peeling pagoda the five hundred tons
of hermaphrodite Word?

At the inn I prepare to surrender again my defeated
shoes to the bending maid   But suddenly the closed
lotus opens to a smile and she points
over my shoulder   above the sagging tiles   to where
tall in the bare sky and huge as Gulliver
a carp is rising   golden and fighting
thrusting its paper body up from the fist
of a small boy on an empty roof   higher
and higher   into the endless winds of the world

Kyoto & Hong Kong 1958

The Bear on the Delhi Road

Unreal   tall as a myth
by the road the Himalayan bear
is beating the brilliant air
with his crooked arms
About him two men   bare
spindly as locusts   leap

One pulls on a ring
in the great soft nose   His mate
flicks   flicks with a stick
up at the rolling eyes

They have not led him here
down from the fabulous hills
to this bald alien plain
and the clamorous world   to kill
but simply to teach him to dance

They are peaceful both   these spare
men of Kashmir   and the bear
alive is their living   too
If   far on the Delhi way
around him galvanic they dance
it is merely to wear   wear
from his shaggy body the tranced
wish forever to stay
only an ambling bear
four-footed in berries

It is no more joyous for them
in this hot dust to prance
out of reach of the praying claws

sharpened to paw for ants
in the shadows of deodars
It is not easy to free
myth from reality
or rear this fellow up
to lurch   lurch with them
in the tranced dancing of men

Srinagar 1958—Île des Porquerolles 1959

For George Lamming

To you
        I can risk words about this

Mastering them   you know
        they are dull
                servants
who say less
        and worse
                than we feel

That party above Kingston Town
        we stood   five (six?) couples

linked singing
        more than rum happy

I was giddy
        from sudden friendship
wanted   undeserved

        black tulip faces
self swaying forgotten
        laughter in dance

Suddenly on a wall mirror
    my face assaulted me
stunned to see itself
    like a white snail
        in the supple dark flowers

Always now I move grateful
    to all of you
who let me walk thoughtless
    and unchallenged
in the gardens
    in the castles
        of your skins

Kingston, Jamaica 1962

ARRIVALS   Wolfville
Locals
From Halifax   30 mins L

It was the hand that caught in me

Sudden as a beast the blizzard
had whirled on us   was gone
as quick over the hill and howling
through the next village   whose spire
could be glimpsed blotting out now
in a grey fury

And we are wading   a straggle of passengers
in town shoes   through a snowscape
clean and cosy as any Christmas card
the small firs like spunwhite candy
spaced on the ice-cream hillocks

Already the sunlight quivers down
burning on the narrow tracks at the crossing
and fires the sleet that sheathes one flank
and the bland diesel-face of our train
so small and innocent now it has stopped

You wouldnt think from that little jolt we got!
. . . Speedin . . . Naw, in that storm he jes couldn see

   Green as a great bruise
   where the smooth flesh of the drifts
   has been savaged   the auto lies
   crumpled and akimbo
   like a beetle battered by catspaw

Flung it fifty feet . . . Yeah an him further . . .
This year's chevvy . . . Well we stopped fast enough

   We stand   the unsilent   stamping
   staring   to reduce to livable size
   what is casually spreadeagled here in the snow

Should be a law about level cross—
Sure but we oughta wistled wen—Hell we did!
. . . Anybody know who he is?

   We too anonymous   one to the other
   but our breaths write on the air
   the kinship of being alive
   surrounding the perfect stranger

Christ it's too cold I'm gittin back . . .
Yep ain't nothin we kin do . . . Hey look
he's only gone three hunderd . . .

   A thin man unprompted is gathering papers
   slewed from a briefcase over the raddled banks
   He slaps them free of flakes ·

and packs them carefully back in the case
Now he teeters   not knowing what to do with it
The brakeman plods up with a plaid blanket

Train gonna be held up till police come?
. . . No I'm stayin
Conductor was up to that farm phonin em

The man with the case silently lays it
next to the open palm
the blanket has failed to cover
He offers his only remark

Assizes is on up to Wolfville
Them's law papers

The halfburied engine continues to tick
with cooling   something live under the snow
Each time we are startled

Lawyer eh? . . . Musta stalled on the track
grabbed his case   got half out his door . . .
Yep   nearly made it . . . Young feller too

The sun has given way again to a black sky
Most have tramped back to the train
The rest of us circle about
as if for somewhere to put down the guilt

Yer all lucky we dint go offa the tracks
. . . He's right   Can't blame the crew none

Diesel shrieks and we jump
The brakeman gestures   Turning at once
we leave him beating his arms for warmth
turn in a pleasure of hurry   to hop
like schoolboys back in the steps we made
eager for heat and motion   arrivals
and shaping already what happened

The train moves to its goal
and scatters us from the scene forever
The manner of hills   words   faces
slides from the gloss protecting each mind
We will forget even that scotched face perhaps
waiting till the gay rug came down
in a Christmas world

But not surely the longfingered hand
stretched in some arresting habit of eloquence
to the last irrational judgement
roaring in from the storm

Or is it only in me that the hand hooked
and I who must manage it now like a third?

1962

Cartagena de Indias

'Ciudad triste, ayer reina de la mar.'—HEREDIA

Each face its own phantom
its own formula of breed and shade
but all the eyes accuse me back and say

There are only two races here:
we human citizens
who are poor but have things to sell
and you   from outer space
unseasonable   our one tourist
but plainly able to buy

This arthritic street
where Drake's men and Cole's ran
swung cutlasses   where wine and sweet blood

snaked in the cobble's joints
        leaps now in a sennet of taxi horns
        to betray my invasion
All watch my first retreat
to barbizans patched from Morgan's grapeshot
and they rush me
        three desperate tarantula youths
        waving Old Golds unexcised

By an altar blackened
where the Indian silver was scratched away
in sanctuary leaning   on lush cool marble
        I am hemmed by a Congo drum man in jeans
    He bares a brace of Swiss watches
        whispers in husky Texan

Where gems and indigo were sorted
        in shouting arcades
        I am deftly shortchanged
and slink to the trees that lean
and flower tall in the Plaza
        Nine shoeboys wham their boxes
        slap at my newshined feet

Only in the Indio market
mazed on the sodden quais
I am granted uneasy truce
Around the ritual braidings of hair
the magical arrangements of fish
the piled rainbows of rotting fruit
I cast a shadow of silence
        blue-dreaded eyes
        corpse face
        hidalgo clothes
        tall one   tall as a demon
        pass O pass us quickly

Behind me the bright blaze of patois
        leaps again

I step to the beautiful slave-built bridge
and a mestiza girl
        levels Christ's hands at me
        under a dangling goitre

Past the glazed-eyed screamers of *dulces*
swing to a pink lane
where a poxed and slit-eyed savage
        pouts an obscenity
        offering a sister
        as he would spit me
        a dart from a blowpipe

Somewhere there must be another bridge
from my stupid wish
to their human acceptance
but what can I offer—
my tongue half-locked in the cell
of its language—other than pesos
        to these old crones of thirty
        whose young sink in pellagra
        as I clump unmaimed
        in the bright shoes
        that keep me from hookworm
        lockjaw and snakebite

It's written in the cut of my glasses
I've a hotelroom all to myself
with a fan   and a box of Vitamin C
It can be measured
in my unnatural stride
that my life expectation
is more than forty
especially now that I'm close to sixty

older than ever bankrupt Bolívar was
who sits now in a frozen prance
high over the coconut trays
quivering on the heads
  of three gaunt mulatto ladies
  circling in a pavane of commerce
  down upon spotlit me

Out of the heaving womb of independence
Bolívar rode and over the bloody afterbirth
into coffee and standard oil
  from inquisitional baroque
  to armed forces corbusier
He alone has nothing more to sell me

I come routed now scuffling
through dust in a nameless square
treeless burning deserted
come lost and guiltily wakeful
in the hour of siesta
  at last to a message

  to a pair of shoes
  in a circle of baked mud
  worn out of shape one on its side
For a second I am shaken by panic
heat? humidity? something has got me
  the shoes are concrete
  and ten feet long

  the sight of a plaque calms
  without telling me much

*En homenaje de la **memoria** de*
LUIS LOPEZ
se erigió este monumento
a los zapatos viejos
el día 10 de febrero de 1957

Luis Lopez?   Monument to his old shoes?
What???   There was nothing else

Back through the huckster streets
the sad taxi men still awake and horn-happy

> *Si señor   Luis Lopez el poeta*
> Here is his book
> Unamuno praised it   *si si*
> You have seen *los zapatos?*   Ah?
> But they are us, *señor*
> It was about us he wrote
> about Cartagena where he was born
> and died   See here this sonnet
> always he made hard words
> Said we were lazy except to make noise
> we only shout to get money
> ugly too, backward . . . why not?
> It is for a poet to write these things
> Also *plena*—how say it?—
> *plena de rancio desaliño*
Full of rancid disarray!
> *Si si* but look, at the end, when old
> he come to say one nice thing
> only one ever about us
> He say we inspire that love a man has
> for his old shoes—*Entonces*
> we give him a monument to the shoes

I bought the book   walked back
sat on the curb happier than Wordsworth
gazing away at his daffodils
Discarded queen   I thought   I love you too
Full of rancid disarray
city like any city
full of the stench of human indignity
and disarray of the human proportion
full of the noisy always poor

and the precocious dying
stinking with fear   the stale of ignorance
I love you first for giving birth
to Luis Lopez   suffering him
honouring him at last
in the grand laconic manner
he taught you

—and him I envy
I who am seldom read by my townsmen

Descendants of pirates   grandees
galleyslaves and cannibals
I love the whole starved cheating
poetry-reading lot of you   most of all
for throwing me the shoes of deadman Luis
to walk me back into your brotherhood

Colombia 1962—Greece 1963

November Walk Near False Creek Mouth

The time is the last of warmth
and the fading of brightness
    before the final flash and the night

I walk as the earth turns
from its burning father
here on this lowest edge of mortal city
where windows flare on faded flats
and the barren end of the ancient English
    who tippled mead in Alfred's hall
    and took tiffin in lost Lahore
drink now their fouroclock chainstore tea
sighing like old pines as the wind turns

The beat is the small   slap   slapping
of the tide sloping   slipping
its long soft fingers into the tense
joints of the trapped seawall

More ones than twos on the beaches today
strolling   or stranded as nations
woolly mermaids   dazed on beachlogs
a kept dog   sniffing   leading his woman
Seldom the lovers   seldom as reason
They will twine indoors from now to May
or ever to never   except the lovers
of what is not city   the refugees
     from the slow volcano
     the cratered rumbling   sirening vents
     the ashen air   the barren spilling
     compulsive rearing of glassy cliff
     from city
they come to the last innocent warmth
and the fading
before the unimaginable brightness

The theme lies in the layers
made and unmade by the nudging   lurching
spiralling down from nothing

down through the common explosion of time
through the chaos of suns
to the high seas of the spinning air
where the shelves form   and re-form down
through cirrus to clouds on cracking peaks
to the terraced woods and the shapeless town
and its dying shapers

The act is the sliding out
to the shifting rotting
folds of the sands that lip
slipping to reefs and sinking cliffs

that ladder down to the ocean's abyss
and farther down through a thousand seas
of the mantling rock
to the dense unbeating black unapproachable
heart of this world

Lanknosed lady sits on a seawall
not alone   she sits with an older book
Who is it?   Shakespeare   Sophocles   Simenon?
They are tranced as sinners unafraid
in the common gaze to pursue
under hard covers their private quaint barren
affair   though today there is no unbusy body
but me to throw them a public look

　　not this wrinkled triad of tourists
　　strayed off the trail from the rank zoo
　　peering away from irrelevant sea
　　seeking a starred sign for the bus-stop
　　They dangle plastic totems   a kewpie
　　a Hong Kong puzzle for somebody's child
　　who waits to be worshipped
　　back on the prairie farm

　　No nor the two manlings
　　all muscles and snorkels and need to shout
　　with Canadian voices   Nipponese bodies
　　racing each other into the chilling waters
　　last maybe of whatever summer's swimmers

　　Nor for certain the gamey old gaffer
　　asleep on the bench like a local Buddha
　　above them   buttonedup mackinaw
　　Sally Ann trousers   writing in stillness
　　his own last book   under the squashed
　　cock of his hat   with a bawdy plot
　　she never will follow

A tremor only of all his dream
runs like fear from under the hat
through the burned face to twitch
one broken boot   at the other end
of the bench as I pass

dreaming my own unraveled plots
between eating water and eaten shore
    in this hour of the tired and homing
    retired   dissolving
    in the days of the separate wait
    for the mass dying

and I   having clambered down to the last
shelf of the gasping world of lungs
do not know why I too wait   and stare
before descending the final step
into the clouds of the sea

The beat beating   is the soft cheek
nudging of the sly   shoving   almost
immortal ocean at work
on the earth's liquidation

Outward the sun   explodes light
like a mild rehearsal of light to come
over the vitreous waters
At this edge of the blast
a young girl sits on a granite bench
so still as if already only
silhouette burned in the stone

Two women pass in a cloud of words
    ... so I said   You're *not*!?
    and she said   I *am*!
    I'm one of the Lockeys!
    Not the Lockeys of *Out*garden surely
    I said   *Yes*   she said   but I live

in Winnipeg now   Why for heaven's *sake*
I said   then you *must* know Carl *Thor*son?
Carl? she said   he's my cousin by marriage
He *is*   I said   why he's *mine* too! So . . .

Born from the glare come the freakish forms
of tugs   all bows and swollen funnels
straining to harbor in False Creek
and blindly followed by mute scows
    with islets of gravel to thicken the city
    and square bowls of saffron sawdust
        the ground meal of the manstruck forest
or towing shining grids of the trees stricken

At the edge of knowledge the *Prince Apollo*
    (or is it the *Princess Helen?*)
floats in a paperblue fusion of air
gulf   Mykenean islands
and crawls with its freight of flesh
toward the glare and the night waiting
behind the hidden Gate of the Lions

The beat is the slap slip   nudging
as the ledges are made   unmade
by the lurching swaying of all the world
that lies under the spinning air

from the dead centre and the fiery circles
up through the ooze to black liquidities
up to the vast moats
where the doomed whales are swimming
by the weedy walls of sunless Carcassonnes
rising   rising   to the great eels waiting
in salt embrasures   and swirling up
to the twilit roofs that floor the Gulf
up to the crab-scratched sands
of the dappled Banks

into the sunblazed living mud
and the radiant mussels
that armor the rocks

    and I on the path at the high-tide edge
    wandering under the leafless maples
    between the lost salt home
    and the asphalt ledge where carhorns call
    call in the clotting air by a shore
    where shamans never again will sound
    with moon-snail conch the ritual plea
    to brother salmon or vanished seal
    and none ever heard
    the horn of Triton or merman

The beat is the bob   dip   dipping
in the small waves   of the ducks shoring
and the shored rocks that seem to move
from turning earth or breathing ocean
in the dazzling slant of the cooling sun

Through piled backyards of the sculptor sea
I climb   over discarded hemlock saurians
    Medusae cedar-stumps   muscled horsemen
    Tartars or Crees   sandsunk forever
and past the raw sawed butt
    telltale with brands
of a buccaneered boom-log
    whisked away to a no-question mill

all the swashing topmost reach of the sea
    that is also the deepest
    reach of wrens   the vanishing squirrel
    and the spilling city
the stinking ledge disputed by barnacles
waiting for tiderise to kick in their food
contested by jittery sandfleas
and hovering gulls that are half-sounds only

traced overhead   lone as my half-thoughts
   wheeling too with persistence of hunger
   or floating on scraps of flotsam

Slowly   scarcely sensed   the beat
has been quickening now as the air
from the whitened peaks is falling
faraway sliding   pouring down
through the higher canyons and over
knolls and roofs to a oneway urgent
procession of rhythms

blowing the haze from False Creek's girders
where now I walk as the waves stream
from my feet to the bay to the far shore
Where they lap like dreams that never reach

The tree-barbed tip of Point Grey's lance
has failed again to impale the gone sun
Clouds and islands float together
out from the darkening bandsaw of suburbs
and burn like sodium over the sunset waters

Something   is it only the wind?
above a jungle of harbor masts
is playing paperchase with the persons
of starlings   They sift and fall
stall and soar   turning
   as I too turn   with the need to feel
   once more the yielding of moist sand
   and thread the rocks back to the seawall

shadowed and empty now
of booklost ladies or flickering wrens

   and beyond to the Boats for Hire
   where a thin old Swede clings in his chair
   like hope to the last light
   eyeing bluely the girls with rackets

padding back from belated tennis
while herring gulls make civic statues
of three posts on the pier
and all his child-bright boats
heave unwanted to winter sleep

Further the shore dips   and the sea   sullen
with sludge from floors of barges   spits
arrogantly over the Harbour Board's wall
and only the brutish prow of something
a troller perhaps   lies longdrowned
on an Ararat of broken clamshells
and the flakings of dead crabs

The shore snouts up again
spilling beachlogs glossy and dry
as sloughed snakeskins
but with sodden immovable hearts
heigh ho the logs that no one wants
and the men that sit on the logs
that no one wants
while the sea repeats what it said
to the first unthinking frogs
and the green wounds of the granite stones

By cold depths and by cliffs
whose shine will pass any moment now
the shore puts an end to my ledge
and I climb past the dried shell
of the children's pool   waiting like faith
for summer   to where the last leaves
of the shore's alders   glistening with salt
have turned the ragged lawns
to a battlefield bright with their bodies

For the time is after the scarring of maples
torn by the fall's first fury of air
on the nearest shelf above brine and sand
where the world of the dry troubling begins

the first days of the vitreous fusing
of deserts   the proud irradiations of air
in the time when men rise
and fall   from the moon's ledge

while the moon sends   as before
the waters swirling up and back
from the bay's world
to this darkening bitten shore

I turn to the terraced road
the cold steps to the bland new block
the human-encrusted reefs
that rise here higher than firs or singing
up to aseptic penthouse hillforts
to antennae above the crosses
pylons marching over the peaks
of mountains without Olympus

Higher than clouds and strata of jetstreams
the air-roads wait the two-way traffic
And beyond?   The desert planets
What else?   a galaxy-full perhaps
of suns and penthouses waiting

But still on the highest shelf of ever
washed by the curve of timeless returnings
lies the unreached unreachable nothing
whose winds wash down to the human shores
and slip   shoving

into each thought nudging my footsteps now
as I turn to my brief night's ledge

in the last of warmth
and the fading of brightness
on the sliding edge of the beating sea

Vancouver 1961—Ametlla, Spain 1963

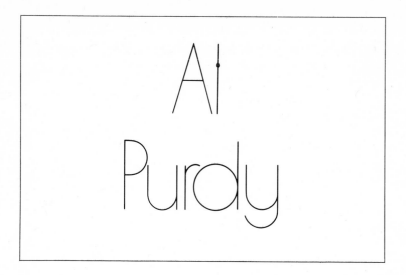

The Cariboo Horses

At 100 Mile House the cowboys ride in rolling
stagey cigarettes with one hand reining
half-tame bronco rebels on a morning grey as stone
—so much like riding dangerous women
            with whiskey coloured eyes—
such women as once fell dead with their lovers
with fire in their heads and slippery froth on thighs
—Beaver and Carrier women maybe or
            Blackfoot squaws far past the edge of this valley
on the other side of those two toy mountain ranges
            from the sunfierce plains beyond—

But only horses
                waiting in stables
hitched at taverns
                standing at dawn
pastured outside the town with
jeeps and fords and chevvys and
busy muttering stake trucks rushing

importantly over roads of man's devising
over the safe known roads of the ranchers
families and merchants of the town—
         On the high prairie
are only horse and rider
         wind in dry grass
clopping in silence under the toy mountains
dropping sometimes and
         lost in the dry grass
         golden oranges of dung—

Only horses
         no stopwatch memories or palace ancestors
not Kiangs hauling undressed stone in the Nile Valley
and having stubborn Egyptian tantrums or
Onagers racing thru Hither Asia and
the last Quagga screaming in African highlands
         lost relatives of these
         whose hooves were thunder
the ghosts of horses battering thru the wind
whose names were the wind's common usage
whose life was the sun's
         arriving here at chilly noon
         in the gasoline smell of the
         dust and waiting 15 minutes
         at the grocer's—

Song of the Impermanent Husband

Oh I would
         I would in a minute
if the cusswords and bitter anger couldn't—
if the either/or quarrel didn't—
and the fat around my middle wasn't—
if I was young if
         I wasn't so damn sure

I couldn't find another maddening bitch
like you holding on for dear life to
all the different parts of me for
twenty or twenty
                    thousand years
I'd leave in the night like
a disgraced caviar salesman
                    descend the moonlight
stairs to Halifax
        (uh—no—not Halifax)
well then Toronto
                    uh
I guess not Toronto either/or
nouveau riche Vancouver down
                                down
                                        down
the dark stairs to
the South Seas' sunlit milky reefs and
        the jungle's green
                    unending bank account with
all the brown girls being brown
                    as they can be and all
the one piece behinds stretched tight tonight
in small sarongs not to be touched tho Oh
beautiful as an angel's ass without the genitals
and me
        in Paris like a smudged Canadian postcard and
(dear me)
        all the importuning white and lily girls
of Rue Pigalle
            and stroll
the sodden London streets and
            find a sullen foggy woman who
enjoyed my odd colonial ways and send
a postcard back to you about my faithfulness and
talk about the lovely beastly English weather
I'd be the slimiest most uxorious wife deserter
            my shrunk amoeba self absurd inside

a saffron girl's geography and
hating me between magnetic nipples
but
    fooling no one in all the sad
    and much emancipated world
Why then I'll stay at least for tea for
all the brownness is too brown and
all the whiteness too damned white
and I'm afraid
        afraid of being
any other woman's man who
might be me
       afraid
the unctuous and uneasy self I glimpse
sometimes might lose my faint and yapping cry for
being anything was never quite what I intended
And you you
       bitch no irritating
questions re love and permanence only
       an unrolling lifetime here
between your rocking thighs and
       the semblance of motion

Transient

Riding the boxcars out of Winnipeg in a
morning after rain so close to
the violent sway of fields it's
like running and running
naked with summer in your mouth and
the guy behind you grunts and says
'Got a smoke?'

Being a boy scarcely a moment and you
hear the rumbling iron roadbed singing
under the wheels at night and a door jerking open

mile after dusty mile riding into Regina with
the dust storm crowding behind you and
a guy you hardly even spoke to
nudges your shoulder chummily and says
'Got a smoke?'

Riding into the Crow's Nest mountains with
your first beard itching and a
hundred hungry guys fanning out thru
the shabby whistlestops for handouts and
not even a sandwich for two hundred miles
only the high mountains and knowing
what it's like to be not quite a child
any more and listening to the tough men
talk of women and talk of the way things are
in 1937

Riding down in the spit-grey sea level morning
thru dockyard streets and dingy dowager houses
with ocean a jump away and the sky beneath you
in puddles on Water Street and an old Indian woman
pushing her yawning scratching daughter
onto a balcony to yell at the boy-man passing
'Want some fun?—come on up' and the girl just
come from riding the shrieking bedspring bronco
all the up and down night to a hitchpost morning
full of mothers and dirt and lice and
            hardly the place for a princess
            of the Coast Salish
                        (My dove my little one
tonight there will be wine and the loins of a dozen men
to pin you down in the outlying lands of sleep
innocent as a child
            awaiting the last of all your bridegrooms)

Stand in the swaying boxcar doorway
moving east away from the sunset and
after a while the eyes digest a country and

the belly perceives a mapmaker's vision
in dust and dirt on the face and hands here
its smell drawn deep thru the nostrils down
to the lungs and spurts thru blood stream
campaigns in the lower intestine
            and chants love songs to the kidneys
After a while there is no arrival and
no departure possible any more
you are where you were always going
and the shape of home has planted itself in your loins
the identity of forests that were always nameless
the selfhood of rivers that are changing always
the nationality of riding a boxcar thru the depression
over long green plains and high mountain country
with the best and worst of a love that's not to be spoken
and a guy right behind you says then
'Got a smoke?'
You give him one and stand in the boxcar doorway
or looking out the window of a Montreal apartment
or running the machines in a Vancouver factory
—you stand there growing older

Eskimo Graveyard

Walking in glacial litter
frost boils and boulder pavements
of an old river delta
where angry living water
changes its mind every half century
and takes a new direction
to the blue fiord
The Public Works guy I'm with
says you always find good gravel
for concrete near a graveyard
where digging is easy maybe
a footnote on human character

But wrapped in blankets
above ground a dead old woman
(for the last few weeks I'm told)
without a grave marker
And a hundred yards away
the Anglican missionary's grave
with whitewashed cross
that means equally nothing
The river's soft roar
drifts to my ears and changes
tone when the wind changes
ice debris melts at low tide
& the Public Works guy is mildly pleased
with the good gravel we found
for work on the schoolhouse
which won't have to be shipped in
from Montreal
and mosquitoes join happily
in our conversation   Then
he stops to consult
with the construction foreman
I walk on
toward the tents of The People
half a mile away
at one corner of the picture
Mothers with children on their backs
in the clean white parkas
they take such pride in
buying groceries at H.B.C.
boys lounging under the store
in space where timber stilts
hold it above the permafrost
with two of them arm in arm
in the manner of Eskimo friends
After dinner
I walk down among the tents
and happen to think of the old woman
neither wholly among the dead

nor quite gone from the living
and wonder how often
a thought of her enters the minds
of people she knew before
and what kind of flicker it is
as lights begin to come on
in nightlong twilight
and thoughts of me
occur to the mosquitoes
I keep walking
as if something ought to happen
(I don't know what)
with the sun stretching
a yellow band across the water
from headland to black headland
at high tide in the fiord
sealing in the settlement
as if there was no way out
and indeed there isn't
until the looping Cansos come
dropping thru the mountain doorway
That old woman?
it occurs to me
I might have been thinking
about human bookkeeping
debits and credits that is
or profit and loss
(and laugh at myself)
among the sealed white tents
like glowing swans
hoping
for a most improbable
birth

Pangnirtung

Arctic Rhododendrons

They are small purple surprises
in the river's white racket
and after you've seen them
a number of times
in water-places
where their silence seems
related to river-thunder
you think of them as 'noisy flowers'
Years ago
it may have been
that lovers came this way
stopped in the outdoor hotel
to watch the water floorshow
and lying prone together
where the purged green
boils to a white heart
and the shore trembles
like a stone song
with bodies touching
flowers were their conversation
and love the sound of a colour
that lasts two weeks in August
and then dies
except for the three or four
I pressed in a letter
and sent whispering to you

Pangnirtung

Detail

The ruined stone house
has an old apple tree
left there by the farmer

whatever else he took with him
It bears fruit every year
gone wild and wormy
with small bitter apples
nobody eats
even children know better
I passed that way on the road
to Trenton twice a month
all winter long
noticing how the apples clung
in spite of hurricane winds
sometimes with caps of snow
little golden bells
And perhaps none of the other
travellers looked that way
but I make no parable of them
they were there and that's all
For some reason I must remember
and think of the leafless tree
and its fermented fruit
one week in late January
when wind blew down the sun
and earth shook like a cold room
no one could live in
with zero weather
soundless golden bells
alone in the storm

Interruption

When the new house was built
callers came:
black squirrels on the roof every morning
between sleep and wakefulness,
and a voice saying 'Hello dead man.'

A chipmunk looks in the window
and I look out,
the small face and the large one
waver together in glass,
but neither moves
while the leaves turn into shadows.
Orioles, robins and red-winged blackbirds
are crayons that colour the air;
something sad and old
cries down in the swamp.
Moonlight in the living room,
a row of mice single file
route marching across the empty lunar plain
until they touch one of my thoughts
and jump back frightened,
but I don't wake up.
Pike in the lake pass and re-pass the windows
with clouds in their mouth.
For 20 minutes every night
the sun slaps a red paint brush
over dinner dishes and leftovers,
but we keep washing it off.
Birds can't take a short cut home,
they have to fly around the new house;
and cedars grow pale green candles
to light their way thru the dark.
Already the house is old:
a drowned chipmunk (the same one?)
in the rain barrel this morning,
dead robins in the roof overhang,
and the mice are terrified—
We have set traps,
and must always remember
to avoid them ourselves.

Lament for the Dorsets

(Eskimos extinct in the 14th century A.D.)

Animal bones and some mossy tent rings
scrapers and spearheads   carved ivory swans
all that remains of the Dorset giants
who drove the Vikings back to their long ships
talked to spirits of earth and water
—a picture of terrifying old men
so large they broke the backs of bears
so small they lurk behind bone rafters
in the brain of modern hunters
among good thoughts and warm things
and come out at night
to spit on the stars

The big men with clever fingers
who had no dogs and hauled their sleds
over the frozen northern oceans
awkward giants
                        killers of seal
they couldn't compete with little men
who came from the west with dogs
Or else in a warm climatic cycle
the seals went back to cold waters
and the puzzled Dorsets scratched their heads
with hairy thumbs around 1350 A.D.
—couldn't figure it out
went around saying to each other
plaintively
                'What's wrong? What happened?
                Where are the seals gone?'
And died

Twentieth century people
apartment dwellers
executives of neon death
warmakers with things that explode

—they have never imagined us in their future
how could we imagine them in the past
squatting among the moving glaciers
six hundred years ago
with glowing lamps?
As remote or nearly
as the trilobites and swamps
when coal became
or the last great reptile hissed
at a mammal the size of a mouse
that squeaked and fled

Did they ever realize at all
what was happening to them?
Some old hunter with one lame leg
a bear had chewed
sitting in a caribou skin tent
—the last Dorset?
Let's say his name was Kudluk
carving 2-inch ivory swans
for a dead grand-daughter
taking them out of his mind
the places in his mind
where pictures are
He selects a sharp stone tool
to gouge a parallel pattern of lines
on both sides of the swan
holding it with his left hand
bearing down and transmitting
his body's weight
from brain to arm and right hand
and one of his thoughts
turns to ivory
The carving is laid aside
in beginning darkness
at the end of hunger
after a while wind
blows down the tent and snow

begins to cover him
After 600 years
the ivory thought
is still warm

The Runners

'It was when Leif was with King Olaf Tryggvason, and he bade him pro-
claim Christianity to Greenland, that the king gave him two Gaels; the
man's name was Haki, and the woman's Haekia. The king advised Leif to
have recourse to these people, if he should stand in need of fleetness, for
they were swifter than deer. Erick and Leif had tendered Karlsefni the
services of this couple. Now when they had sailed past Marvel-Strands
(to the New World) they put the Gaels ashore, and directed them to run
to the southward, and investigate the nature of the country, and return
again before the end of the third half-day.'

—From ERICK THE RED'S SAGA

Brother, the wind of this place is cold,
and hills under our feet tremble,
the forests are making magic against us—
I think the land knows we are here,
I think the land knows we are strangers.
Let us stay close to our friend the sea,
or cunning dwarves at the roots of darkness
shall seize and drag us down—

Sister, we must share our strength between us,
until the heat of our bodies makes a single flame,
and one that we are is more than two that we were:
while the moon sees only one shadow,
and the sun knows only our double heartbeat,
and the rain does not come between—

Brother, I am afraid of this dark place,
I am hungry for the home islands,
and wind blowing the waves to coloured spray,
I am sick for the sun—

Sister, we must not think those thoughts again,
for three half-days have gone by,
and we must return to the ship.
If we are away longer,
the Northmen will beat us with thongs,
until we cry for death—
Why do you stare at nothing?

Brother, a cold wind touched me,
tho I stand in your arms' circle:
perhaps the Northmen's runes have found us,
the runes they carve on wood and stone.
I am afraid of this dark land,
ground mist that makes us half ghosts,
and another silence inside silence . . .
But there are berries and fish here,
and small animals by the sea's edge
that crouch and tremble and listen . . .
If we join our words to the silence,
if our trails cross the trails we made,
and the sun remembers what the moon forgets . . .
Brother, it comes to me now,
the long ship must sail without us,
we stay here—

Sister, we should die slowly,
the beasts would gnaw at our bodies,
the rains whiten our bones.
The Northmen's runes are strong magic,
the runes would track us down,
tho we keep on running
past the Land of Flat Stones
over the Marvel-Strands
beyond the land of great trees . . .
Tho we ran to the edge of the world,
our masters would track us down—

Brother, take my hand in your hand,
this part of ourselves between us

while we run together,
over the stones of the sea-coast,
this much of ourselves is our own:
while rain cries out against us,
and darkness swallows the evening,
and morning moves into stillness,
and mist climbs to our throats,
while we are running,
while we are running—

Sister—

The Beavers of Renfrew

By day
chain saws stencil the silence in my head,
black quotes appear on the red brain—
Across glacial birth marks old Jake
Loney is cutting his winter wood,
tongue drowned in a chaw of tobacco—
The belly button pond at one
end of the farm brims
full its cockleshell three acres:
—tonight the beaver are back,
and work their swing shift
under the moon.
Sometimes at low earthen dams
where the pouring spillway empties,
they stand upright in a pride of being,
holding rainbow trout like silver thoughts,
or pale gold Indian girls
arriving here intact from bone cameras
ten thousand ancestors ago,
before letting them spin down the moonlight
rapids as mortal lures
for drowned fishermen—
Among the beaver lodges

I stand unable to sleep,
but cannot stay awake
while poplar and birch fall around me.
I am not mistaken for a tree,
but almost totally ignored,
pissed on by mistake occasionally—
Standing here long enough,
seeing the gentle bodies moving
close to what they truly are,
I wonder what screwed-up philosophy,
what claim to a god's indulgence,
made men decide their own importance?
And what is great music and art
but an alibi for murderers?
Perhaps in the far-off beginnings
of things they made a pact with men,
dammed the oceans for us,
chewed a hole in the big log bridge
wedged between Kamchatka and Alaska,
tore open the Mediterranean,
parted the Red Sea for Moses,
drowned Atlantis and the Eden-myth,
original sin and all that,
in the great salt womb of the sea—
And why?
Because they pitied men.
To the wet animal shivering in a tree
they said,
            'Come on down—
                        It's all right.'
And he shinnied down with hairless
purple behind pointed east for heat,
tail between hind legs,
humbly standing on all fours,
touching his forelock muttering,
'Yessir yessir thank'ee kindly,'
but not knowing how to speak yet of course—
Beaver looked at this dripping creature,

a miserable biological dead end:
but every failure has flashes of genius
exploding out of death:
and the man listened
to an agreement of the water beings
and land beings together
which men have forgotten since:
the secret of staying completely still,
allowing ourselves to catch up
with the shadow just ahead of us
we have lost,
when the young world was a cloudy room
drifting thru morning stillness—
But the rest of it
I have forgotten,
and the gentle beaver will not remind us:
standing upright at their earthen dams
holding the moonlit reins of water,
at peace with themselves—

'Why not make a left turn
and just stay here,'
I said next day to old Jake Loney,
'instead of going forward to the planets?'
The chain saw bucked in his hands,
chewing out chunks of pine that toppled
and scarred the air with green absence.
Far off a beaver tail slapped water,
a bird looked for the tree that was gone—
Old Jake's cheek bulged its chaw of tobacco—
'Well, why not?' I said argumentatively,
before he could spit,
                        'Why not?'
And the log bridge across the Bering
burst with a roar around
me again nothing but water,
brown water—
                        'Why not?'

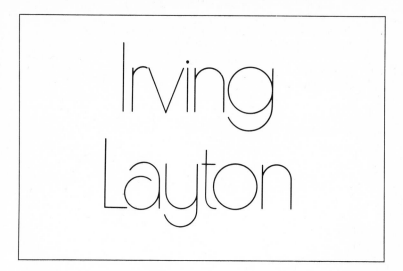

Against This Death

I have seen respectable
death
served up like bread and wine
in stores and offices,
in club and hostel,
and from the streetcorner
church
that faces
two-ways;
I have seen death
served up
like ice.

Against this death,
slow, certain:
the body,
this burly sun,
the exhalations
of your breath,

your cheeks
rose and lovely,
and the secret
life
of the imagination
scheming freedom
from labour
and stone.

Look, the Lambs
Are All Around Us!

Your figure, love,
curves itself
into a man's memory;
or to put it the way
a junior prof
at Mount Allison might,
Helen with her thick
absconding limbs
about the waist
of Paris
did no better.

Hell, my back's sunburnt
from so much love-making
in the open air.
The Primate (somebody
made a monkey of him)
and the Sanhedrin
(long on the beard, short
on the brain)
send envoys to say
they don't approve.
You never see them, love.
You toss me in the air

with such abandon,
they take to their heels and run.
I tell you
each kiss of yours
is like a blow on the head!

What luck, what luck to be loved
by the one girl
in this Presbyterian
country
who knows how to give
a man pleasure.

The Cold Green Element

At the end of the garden walk
the wind and its satellite wait for me;
their meaning I will not know
             until I go there,
but the black-hatted undertaker

who, passing, saw my heart beating in the grass,
is also going there. Hi, I tell him,
a great squall in the Pacific blew a dead poet
             out of the water,
who now hangs from the city's gates.

Crowds depart daily to see it, and return
with grimaces and incomprehension;
if its limbs twitched in the air
             they would sit at its feet
peeling their oranges.

And turning over I embrace like a lover
the trunk of a tree, one of those

for whom the lightning was too much
              and grew a brilliant
hunchback with a crown of leaves.

The ailments escaped from the labels
of medicine bottles are all fled to the wind;
I've seen myself lately in the eyes
              of old women,
spent streams mourning my manhood,

in whose old pupils the sun became
a bloodsmear on broad catalpa leaves
and hanging from ancient twigs,
              my murdered selves
sparked the air like the muted collisions

of fruit. A black dog howls down my blood,
a black dog with yellow eyes;
he too by someone's inadvertence
              saw the bloodsmear
on the broad catalpa leaves.

But the furies clear a path for me to the worm
who sang for an hour in the throat of a robin,
and misled by the cries of young boys
              I am again
a breathless swimmer in that cold green element.

The Fertile Muck

There are brightest apples on those trees
      but until I, fabulist, have spoken
they do not know their significance
or what other legends are hung like garlands
      on their black boughs twisting
like a rumour. The wind's noise is empty.

Nor are the winged insects better off
    though they wear my crafty eyes
wherever they alight. Stay here, my love;
you will see how delicately they deposit
    me on the leaves of elms
or fold me in the orient dust of summer.

And if in August joiners and bricklayers
    are thick as flies around us
building expensive bungalows for those
who do not need them, unless they release
    me roaring from their moth-proofed cupboards
their buyers will have no joy, no ease.

I could extend their rooms for them without cost
    and give them crazy sundials
to tell the time with, but I have noticed
how my irregular footprint horrifies them
    evenings and Sunday afternoons:
they spray for hours to erase its shadow.

How to dominate reality? Love is one way;
    imagination another. Sit here
beside me, sweet; take my hard hand in yours.
We'll mark the butterflies disappearing over the hedge
    with tiny wristwatches on their wings:
our fingers touching the earth, like two Buddhas.

On Seeing the Statuettes
of Ezekiel and Jeremiah in the
Church of Notre Dame

They have given you French names
    and made you captive, my rugged
troublesome compatriots;
    your splendid beards, here, are epicene,

plaster white
        and your angers
unclothed with Palestinian hills quite lost
in this immense and ugly edifice.

You are bored—I see it—sultry prophets
       with priests and nuns
(What coarse jokes must pass between you!)
       and with those morbidly religious
i.e. my prize brother-in-law
                ex-Lawrencian
pawing his rosary, and his wife
sick with many guilts.

Believe me I would gladly take you
       from this spidery church
its bad melodrama, its musty smell of candle
       and set you both free again
in no make-believe world
          of sin and penitence
but the sunlit square opposite
alive at noon with arrogant men.

Yet cheer up Ezekiel and you Jeremiah
       who were once cast into a pit;
I shall not leave you here incensed, uneasy
       among alien Catholic saints
but shall bring you from time to time
         my hot Hebrew heart
as passionate as your own, and stand
with you here awhile in aching confraternity.

Sacrament by the Water

How shall I sing the accomplished waters
Whose teeming cells make green my hopes'
How shall the Sun at daybreak marry us
Twirling these waters like a hoop.

Gift of the waters that sing
Their eternal passion for the sky,
Your cunning beauty in a wave of tumult
Drops an Eden about your thighs.

Green is the singing singing water
And green is every joyous leaf
White myrtle's in your hand and in the other
The hairy apple bringing life.

Whatever Else Poetry Is Freedom

Whatever else poetry is freedom.
Forget the rhetoric, the trick of lying
All poets pick up sooner or later. From the river,
Rising like the thin voice of grey castratos—the mist;
Poplars and pines grow straight but oaks are gnarled;
Old codgers must speak of death, boys break windows;
Women lie honestly by their men at last.

And I who gave my Kate a blackened eye
Did to its vivid changing colours
Make up an incredible musical scale;
And now I balance on wooden stilts and dance
And thereby sing to the loftiest casements.
See how with polish I bow from the waist.
Space for these stilts! More space or I fail!

And a crown I say for my buffoon's head.
Yet no more fool am I than King Canute,
Lord of our tribe, who scanned and scorned;
Who half-deceived, believed; and, poet, missed
The first white waves come nuzzling at his feet;
Then damned the courtiers and the foolish trial
With a most bewildering and unkingly jest.

It was the mist. It lies inside one like a destiny.
A real Jonah it lies rotting like a lung.
And I know myself undone who am a clown
And wear a wreath of mist for a crown;
Mist with the scent of dead apples,
Mist swirling from black oily waters at evening,
Mist from the fraternal graves of cemeteries.

It shall drive me to beg my food and at last
Hurl me broken I know and prostrate on the road;
Like a huge toad I saw, entire but dead,
That Time mordantly had blacked; O pressed
To the moist earth it pled for entry.
I shall be I say that stiff toad for sick with mist
And crazed I smell the odour of mortality.

And Time flames like a paraffin stove
And what it burns are the minutes I live.
At certain middays I have watched the cars
Bring me from afar their windshield suns;
What lay to my hand were blue fenders,
The suns extinguished, the drivers wearing sunglasses.
And it made me think I had touched a hearse.

So whatever else poetry is freedom. Let
Far off the impatient cadences reveal
A padding for my breathless stilts. Swivel,
O hero, in the fleshy groves, skin and glycerine,
And sing of lust, the sun's accompanying shadow
Like a vampire's wing, the stillness in dead feet—
Your stave brings resurrection, O aggrievèd king.

Berry Picking

Silently my wife walks on the still wet furze
Now darkgreen the leaves are full of metaphors
Now lit up is each tiny lamp of blueberry.
The white nails of rain have dropped and the sun is free.

And whether she bends or straightens to each bush
To find the children's laughter among the leaves
Her quiet hands seem to make the quiet summer hush—
Berries or children, patient she is with these.

I only vex and perplex her; madness, rage
Are endearing perhaps put down upon the page;
Even silence daylong and sullen can then
Enamour as restraint or classic discipline.

So I envy the berries she puts in her mouth,
The red and succulent juice that stains her lips;
I shall never taste that good to her, nor will they
Displease her with a thousand barbarous jests.

How they lie easily for her hand to take,
Part of the unoffending world that is hers;
Here beyond complexity she stands and stares
And leans her marvellous head as if for answers.

No more the easy soul my childish craft deceives
Nor the simpler one for whom yes is always yes;
No, now her voice comes to me from a far way off
Though her lips are redder than the raspberries.

Cain

Taking the air rifle from my son's hand,
I measured back five paces, the Hebrew
In me, narcissist, father of children,
Laid to rest. From there I took aim and fired.

The silent ball hit the frog's back an inch
Below the head. He jumped at the surprise
Of it, suddenly tickled or startled
(He must have thought) and leaped from the wet sand
Into the surrounding brown water. But
The ball had done its mischief. His next spring
Was a miserable flop, the thrust all gone
Out of his legs. He tried—like Bruce—again,
Throwing out his sensitive pianist's
Hands as a dwarf might or a helpless child.
His splash disturbed the quiet pondwater
And one old frog behind his weedy moat
Blinking, looking self-complacently on.
The lin's surface at once became closing
Eyelids and bubbles like notes of music
Liquid, luminous, dropping from the page
White, white-bearded, a rapid crescendo
Of inaudible sounds and a crones' whispering
Backstage among the reeds and bulrushes
As for an expiring Lear or Oedipus.

But Death makes us all look ridiculous.
Consider this frog (dog, hog, what you will)
Sprawling, his absurd corpse rocked by the tides
That his last vain spring had set in movement.
Like a retired oldster, I couldn't help sneer,
Living off the last of his insurance:
Billows—now crumbling—the premiums paid.
Absurd, how absurd. I wanted to kill
At the mockery of it, kill and kill
Again—the self-infatuate frog, dog, hog,
Anything with the stir of life in it,
Seeing the dead leaper, Chaplin-footed,
Rocked and cradled in this afternoon
Of tranquil water, reeds, and blazing sun,
The hole in his back clearly visible
And the torn skin a blob of shadow
Moving when the quiet poolwater moved.

O Egypt, marbled Greece, resplendent Rome,
Did you also finally perish from a small bore
In your back you could not scratch? And would
Your mouths open ghostily, gasping out
Among the murky reeds, the hidden frogs,
We climb with crushed spines toward the heavens?

When the next morning I came the same way
The frog was on his back, one delicate
Hand on his belly, and his white shirt front
Spotless. He looked as if he might have been
A comic; tapdancer apologizing
For a fall, or an Emcee, his wide grin
Coaxing a laugh from us for an aside
Or perhaps a joke we didn't quite hear.

Keine Lazarovitch 1870-1959

When I saw my mother's head on the cold pillow,
Her white waterfalling hair in the cheeks' hollows,
I thought, quietly circling my grief, of how
She had loved God but cursed extravagantly his creatures.

For her final mouth was not water but a curse,
A small black hole, a black rent in the universe,
Which damned the green earth, stars and trees in its stillness
And the inescapable lousiness of growing old.

And I record she was comfortless, vituperative,
Ignorant, glad, and much else besides; I believe
She endlessly praised her black eyebrows, their thick weave,
Till plagiarizing Death leaned down and took them for his
    mould.

And spoiled a dignity I shall not again find,
And the fury of her stubborn limited mind;

Now none will shake her amber beads and call God blind,
Or wear them upon a breast so radiantly.

O fierce she was, mean and unaccommodating;
But I think now of the toss of her gold earrings,
Their proud carnal assertion, and her youngest sings
While all the rivers of her red veins move into the sea.

A Tall Man Executes a Jig

I

So the man spread his blanket on the field
And watched the shafts of light between the tufts
And felt the sun push the grass towards him;
The noise he heard was that of whizzing flies,
The whistlings of some small imprudent birds,
And the ambiguous rumbles of cars
That made him look up at the sky, aware
Of the gnats that tilted against the wind
And in the sunlight turned to jigging motes.
Fruitflies he'd call them except there was no fruit
About, spoiling to hatch these glitterings,
These nervous dots for which the mind supplied
The closing sentences from Thucydides,
Or from Euclid having a savage nightmare.

II

Jig jig, jig jig. Like minuscule black links
Of a chain played with by some playful
Unapparent hand or the palpitant
Summer haze bored with the hour's stillness.
He felt the sting and tingle afterwards
Of those leaving their orthodox unrest,
Leaving their undulant excitation
To drop upon his sleeveless arm. The grass,
Even the wildflowers became black hairs

And himself a maddened speck among them.
Still the assaults of the small flies made him
Glad at last, until he saw purest joy
In their frantic jiggings under a hair,
So changed from those in the unrestraining air.

III

He stood up and felt himself enormous.
Felt as might Donatello over stone,
Or Plato, or as a man who has held
A loved and lovely woman in his arms
And feels his forehead touch the emptied sky
Where all antinomies flood into light.
Yet jig jig jig, the haloing black jots
Meshed with the wheeling fire of the sun:
Motion without meaning, disquietude
Without sense or purpose, ephemerides
That mottled the resting summer air till
Gusts swept them from his sight like wisps of smoke.
Yet they returned, bringing a bee who, seeing
But a tall man, left him for a marigold.

IV

He doffed his aureole of gnats and moved
Out of the field as the sun sank down,
A dying god upon the blood-red hills.
Ambition, pride, the ecstasy of sex,
And all circumstance of delight and grief,
That blood upon the mountain's side, that flood
Washed into a clear incredible pool
Below the ruddied peaks that pierced the sun.
He stood still and waited. If ever
The hour of revelation was come
It was now, here on the transfigured steep.
The sky darkened. Some birds chirped. Nothing else.
He thought the dying god had gone to sleep:
An Indian fakir on his mat of nails.

V

And on the summit of the asphalt road
Which stretched towards the fiery town, the man
Saw one hill raised like a hairy arm, dark
With pines and cedars against the stricken sun
—The arm of Moses or of Joshua.
He dropped his head and let fall the halo
Of mountains, purpling and silent as time,
To see temptation coiled before his feet:
A violated grass snake that lugged
Its intestine like a small red valise.
A cold-eyed skinflint it now was, and not
The manifest of that joyful wisdom,
The mirth and arrogant green flame of life;
Or earth's vivid tongue that flicked in praise of earth.

VI

And the man wept because pity was useless.
'Your jig's up; the flies come like kites,' he said
And watched the grass snake crawl towards the hedge,
Convulsing and dragging into the dark
The satchel filled with curses for the earth,
For the odours of warm sedge, and the sun,
A blood-red organ in the dying sky.
Backwards it fell into a grassy ditch
Exposing its underside, white as milk,
And mocked by wisps of hay between its jaws;
And then it stiffened to its final length.
But though it opened its thin mouth to scream
A last silent scream that shook the black sky,
Adamant and fierce, the tall man did not curse.

VII

Beside the rigid snake the man stretched out
In fellowship of death; he lay silent
And stiff in the heavy grass with eyes shut,
Inhaling the moist odours of the night
Through which his mind tunnelled with flicking tongue
Backwards to caves, mounds, and sunken ledges
And desolate cliffs where come only kites,
And where of perished badgers and racoons
The claws alone remain, gripping the earth.
Meanwhile the green snake crept upon the sky,
Huge, his mailed coat glittering with stars that made
The night bright, and blowing thin wreaths of cloud
Athwart the moon; and as the weary man
Stood up, coiled above his head, transforming all.

If I Lie Still

If I lie still
the light from the leaves
will drop on my hands and knees

Fire will envelop me
yet I won't burn

I shall hear the silence plainly
while the stream flows into my veins
and out again

Small wild animals will no longer fear me,
but bring their young
to tickle my heels,
nuzzle in my armpits

I shall know love without disquiet
—without passion

For a thousand years
I shall lie like this
with my head toward the sun

Till knowledge and power
have become one;
then I shall write a single verse,
achieve one flawless deed

Then lie down again
to become like this shallow
stone under my hand,
and let my face
be covered with grass

To be pulled out by the roots
by what raging hermit,
his breast torn apart as mine now?

Marché Municipale

FOR DESMOND PACEY

In the empty market
    coolness spills out
from vineyards
    gathered in boxes of grapes;
the rumour of orchards,
and pears full of an indisputable dignity
that lie like jaundiced dowagers
    in their white wrappers;
and from freshly washed tomatoes
that flash in the surrounding gloom
like the neon signs of lost American towns
you speed past on rainy nights
    on the way to nowhere.

It is a coolness
   making herrings smell more rank;
in which the ripe colour of bananas astounds;
potatoes, a visible skin affliction of air,
lie mute, lie sullen in their earthy bags;
and the slow mysterious decay of olives
   filling the deserted aisles
with its black sensual irony discomfits
the pragmatic vegetables in their stands,
   countermands
the imperial fiats of pineapples.

And the stillness is such
   that waits for iron weights or a box
to shatter; or a child hidden
in a cupboard expelling his breath
and saying, 'Ah, Ah' making it appear
   silence had spoken;
or a film with no commentary
showing machine guns and rifles
   fallen out of
the huge blistered hands of destiny
sands are burying; even the muzzles
that with a last malevolent squint
   at the sun
sink into a darkness and silence
more vast, more final than Pharaoh's kingdom.

—poet of Toronto
—joy of recognition — one of the
pleasures of poetry. satis. of meeting the
familiar
—writes about Toronto.

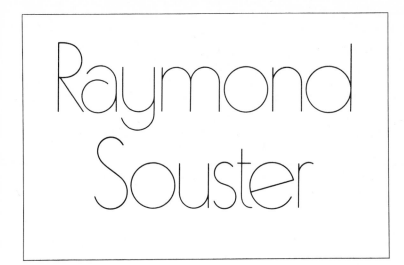

Raymond Souster

The Nest

It will have to be near some water
so there can be moonlight like a pool
to bathe our tired, sleep-returning eyes.

There must be a high, strong roof
so the rain children will not break
the step of their marching above us.

White sheets to lull our flesh asleep
after we've squeezed all the love from our bodies,
with God's hand on the door
so none can touch the slightest scattered hair
of your head on its pillow, that none
will hand me a gun again and say,
leave her, there's new blood to be spilled
in the name of our latest lie.

Young Girls

With the night full of spring and stars we stand
here in this dark doorway and watch the young
girls pass, two, three together, hand in hand.
Like flowers they are whose fragrance has not sprung
or awakened, whose bodies dimly feel
the flooding upward welling of the trees;
whose senses, caressed by the wind's soft fingers, reel
with a delirium that makes them ill at ease.

They lie awake at night unable to sleep
and walk the streets kindled by strange desires;
they steal glances at us, unable to keep
control upon those subterranean fires.
We whistle after them, then laugh, for they
stiffen, not knowing what to do or say.

Lagoons, Hanlan's Point

Mornings
before the sun's liquid
spilled gradually, flooding
the island's cool cellar,
there was the boat
and the still lagoons,
with the sound of my oars
the only intrusion
over cries of birds
in the marshy shallows,
or the loud thrashing
of the startled crane
rushing the air.

And in one strange
dark, tree-hung entrance,
I followed the sound

of my heart all the way
to the reed-blocked ending,
with the pads of the lily
thick as green-shining film
covering the water.

And in another
where the sun came
to probe the depths
through a shaft of branches,
I saw the skeletons
of brown ships rotting
far below in their burial-ground,
and wondered what strange fish
with what strange colours
swam through these palaces
under the water. . . .

A small boy
with a flat-bottomed punt
and an old pair of oars
moving with wonder
through the antechamber
of a waking world.

The Lilac Poem

Before the lilacs are over and they are only
shrunken stalks at the ends of drooping branches,
I want to write a poem about them and their beauty
brief and star-shining as a young girl's promise.

Because there is so much made of strength and wealth and power,
because the little things are lost in this world,
I write this poem about lilacs knowing that both
are this day's only: tomorrow they will lie forgotten.

Free Verse:

Downtown Corner News Stand

specific setting — King & Bay

It will need all of death to take you from this corner.
It has become your world, and you its unshaved
bleary-eyed, foot-stamping king. In winter
you curse the cold, huddled in your coat from the wind,
you fry in summer like an egg hopping on a griddle;
and always the whining voice, the nervous-flinging arms,
the red face, shifting eyes watching, waiting
under the grimy cap for God knows what
to happen. (But nothing ever does, downtown Toronto
goes to sleep and wakes the next morning
always the same, except a little dirtier.)
And you stand with your armful of *Stars* and *Telys*,
the peak of your cap well down against the sun,
and all the city's restless seething river
surges beside you, but not once do you plunge
into its flood, are carried or tossed away:
but reappear always, beard longer than ever, nose running,
to catch the noon editions at King and Bay.

image
love
wheel?
heart/soul
of Toronto

Study: The Bath

In the almost dim light
of the bathroom a woman
steps from white tub
towel around her shoulders.

Drops of water glisten
on her body, slight buttocks,
neck, tight belly,
fall at intervals
from the slightly plumed
oval of crotch.

Neck bent forward
eyes collected
her attention gathered
at the ends of fingers

as she removes
dead skin from her nipples.

Flight of the Roller-Coaster

Once more around should do it, the man confided . . .

and sure enough, when the roller-coaster reached the peak
of the giant curve above me, screech of its wheels
almost drowned out by the shriller cries of the riders,

instead of the dip and plunge with its landslide of screams,
it rose in the air like a movieland magic carpet,
        some wonderful bird,

and without fuss or fanfare swooped slowly across
        the amusement-park,
over Spook's Castle, ice-cream booths, shooting-gallery.
        And losing no height

made the last yards above the beach, where the cucumber-cool
brakeman in the last seat saluted
a lady about to change from her bathing-suit.

Then, as many witnesses reported, headed leisurely
        out over the water,
disappearing all too soon behind a low-flying flight of clouds.

All This Slow Afternoon

All this slow afternoon
the May winds blowing
honey of the lilacs,
sounds of waves washing
through the highest branches
of my poplar tree.

Enough in such hours
to be simply alive;
I will take death tomorrow
without bitterness.

Today all I ask
is to be left alone
in the wind
in the sunshine,
with the honey of lilacs
down the garden;

to fall asleep tired
of small birds' gossip,
of so much greenness
pushed behind my eyes.

The Six-Quart Basket

The six-quart basket
one side gone
half the handle torn off

sits in the centre of the lawn
and slowly fills up
with the white fruits of the snow.

The Death of the Grenadiers

It was over the ice
of this bottomless pond
(so the story goes)
that the Grenadiers
chased those Indians,
and the ice that gave way
to the marching step
of the English held up
for the braves' single file. . . .

And girls have told me
they've felt that someone
was looking up their legs
as they skated the pond,
and looking down they've seen
(noses close to the ice
on the underneath side),
the white-bearded faces
of lonely soldiers
looking up at them
with lascivious winks
in their socketless eyes.

A Morning in Brussels

—Granted the most subtle torture that in which the victim
knows each step of his pain but is powerless to change
it in any way—

Then become this moment the young French-Canadian airman
of twenty, who, having watched in the cellar of the Rue
Royale the most expert monsters of the Gestapo stalk
round on cat-silent shoes behind the line of prisoners
(faces held six inches back from dripping walls), lashing

out with rubber truncheons now at this head and now this,
quite at random, never the same pattern repeated—

Knowing this then stand in line yourself, lips held
tightly together until the first searing terror of your
face smashed against the stone, pain in your nose like
a knife-slit, lips moving tremblingly in prayer, Holy
Mary, Mother of God, as you wait for the warning of
footsteps which never comes, as you wait for an end,
any end. . . .

Memory of Bathurst Street

'Where are you, boy?'
my Aunt Maggie's calling,
but I can't hear her
in my attic eyrie,
where I watch the heat
swirl up from the tar roofs,
and wait for the cry
of the bearded rag-picker
down the lane from Ulster Street.

'Where are you, boy?'
my Uncle Jim's calling,
but I can't hear him
for the cooing of birds
inside this pigeon-house
at the back of the garden,
where I scrape up the droppings
to earn my allowance.

'Where are you, boy?'
my Aunt Lizzie's calling,
but I can't hear her
from the upstairs sitting-room,

as I turn the pages
of my favourite book
where the Highlanders lie
in the blood of their death
on green Spion Kop.

St Catherine Street East

FOR LOUIS DUDEK

Beer on a hot afternoon?—what else
in this Bon Marché of the World,
earth's narrowest, most crowded rabbit-run,
sweating under loud sunshine that glints off
baby carriages, tin cups of beggars,
silver balls of pawnshops, making
the rouge-layered, powder-dipped girls
squint hard but not taking anything off
their free-swinging walk on the stilt-heels.

Beer you said? Right back here
behind giant cheeses, wienerwurst truncheons,
hungry smells of bread, perfumes of coffee.
Look, the cold-sweated bottles count out
to a dozen, and we fight our way
past the check-out counter to the street
where sun, traffic, noise, faces, heat-breath
hit, stun us.
              Every face in every window
of each building watching as we go
down the steaming pavement, on, out of this jungle
where the dead are never buried by the living,
but crowd onto buses, sit late at bar stools, or wait
in the darkness of always airless rooms.

On the Rouge

I can almost see
my father's canoe
pointing in from the lake,
him paddling,
mother hidden
in a hat of fifty years ago.

Turning now up a stream
clear-flowing through marsh
(not mud-brown like today):

gliding under the same
railway bridge we cross under,
slipping by the same giant
stepping-stones of rock
standing up so like ramparts:

moving on to those quieter
summer-singing reaches,
the calling of birds
making speech difficult.

Lost finally, perhaps forever,
behind ferns swallowing banks,
bent trees overarching sky,

drifting the summer
labyrinths of love.

Night Raider

Something getting its Christmas dinner early
in the narrow alley that flanks
our apartment house.
                            Gorging so frantically
it can't hear the noise it makes
rattling trash-can lids, ripping skins
of newspaper-wrapping off the choicest refuse.

This to the sleepy steadiness of rain falling,
so that I get a picture of my animal,
head down in garbage, busy, steam ascending
like a grace from its breathing coat.

Among the Willows

When summer returns, these same willows will
            come alive,
burst bud and throw
a green band along
the mud banks of the river.

When I was a kid, nine or ten years old,
we played our games of cowboys and Indians
among them. More than once surprised
young couples in those thickets,
who, thinking themselves well-hidden,
had abandoned themselves to their loving.

I think we were more
surprised and embarrassed than they were,
for they said nothing to us, made no move
to leave off their pleasure,
while we retreated, confused,
not old or bold enough to know
our easy advantage.

Was it later we collected
soiled sheaths of their mating, spearing them
on the points of sticks?

It may have been.
We had that fresh innocence once,
in the summer, by the river, among the willows.

The First Two Acorns

Only the first two acorns
really counted.

The first,
unhitched from a top branch,
dropped relentlessly through
leaf screens (leaving the air
still shivering behind it)
to strike the road
hard enough to hurt.

The second could have fallen
from any height. All
that the night heard
was a dull plop in grass,
unspectacular to say the least
after that first drop.

Still, it was the one triggered off
tree after tree down the street;
and all on a windless night
with everyone asleep
and only I to ponder
what would happen next
and exactly when.

Get the Poem Outdoors

Get the poem outdoors under any pretext,
reach through the open window if you have to,
     kidnap it right off the poet's desk,
then walk the poem in the garden, hold it up
     among the soft yellow garlands of the
     willow,
command of it no further blackness, no silent
     cursing at midnight, no puny whimpering
     in the endless small hours, no more
     shivering in the cold-storage room of the
     winter heart,
tell it to sing again, loud and then louder so it
     brings the whole neighbourhood out, but
     who cares,
ask of it a more human face, a new tenderness,
     even the sentimental allowed between the
     hours of nine to five,
then let it go, stranger in a fresh green world, to
     wander down the flower beds, let it go to
     welcome each bird that lights on the still
     barren mulberry tree.

The Embarrassment

Granted, the most natural
thing in the world—
                        the new baby cries,
the young mother bares her breast
to feed the greedy monster—

But my shame
coming on you in the kitchen,
unprepared for the great hanging tit,
the suckling infant.
                        So that I mutter
words, any words,
so that I want so desperately to drop
the rye, the ginger ale,
to back out, to hide,
anything but raise my eyes. . . .
And I repeat—this thing you do
the most natural in the world.

So that I know myself
earth's most unnatural,
life's most unprepared fool.
And wonder: how many
of us begin like your infant,
but really never leave the breast,
suck at it
all the innocence of our lives?

46 — Montreal, rich, middle class
- university ed'. — Jewish
- records
- he & his guitar
- novelist.
- love poetry, loosing relationships
- Jewish question? not part of
  Jewish ghetto

Leonard Cohen

[Handwritten annotations:]

fluttering winding sheet –
- Shroud of Torin (city in Italy?)
christ.
- Christ is a man of nature, south,
warm, places, belong to Jewish
people.
went to Jerosofen - crusified - went
to celebrate passover.

- northern christians
- why are you claiming
him a christian - yota
streams - to cold
for him to be
there

kiss - Judas betrayed
christ with a kiss

Elegy

Do not look for him
In brittle mountain streams:
They are too cold for any god;
And do not examine the angry rivers
For shreds of his soft body
Or turn the shore stones for his blood;
But in the warm salt ocean
He is descending through cliffs
Of slow green water
And the hovering coloured fish
Kiss his snow-bruised body
And build their secret nests
In his fluttering winding-sheet.

Story

She tells me a child built her house
one Spring afternoon,
but that the child was killed
crossing the street.

She says she read it in the newspaper,
that at the corner of this and this avenue
a child was run down by an automobile.

Of course I do not believe her.
She has built the house herself,
hung the oranges and coloured beads in the doorways,
crayoned flowers on the walls.
She has made the paper things for the wind,
collected crooked stones for their shadows in the sun,
fastened yellow and dark balloons to the ceiling.

Each time I visit her
she repeats the story of the child to me,
I never question her. It is important
to understand one's part in a legend.

I take my place
among the paper fish and make-believe clocks,
naming the flowers she has drawn,
smiling while she paints my head on large clay coins,
and making a sort of courtly love to her
when she contemplates her own traffic death.

I Have Not Lingered in European Monasteries

I have not lingered in European monasteries
and discovered among the tall grasses tombs of knights
who fell as beautifully as their ballads tell;

I have not parted the grasses
or purposefully left them thatched.

I have not released my mind to wander and wait
in those great distances
between the snowy mountains and the fishermen,
like a moon,
or a shell beneath the moving water.

I have not held my breath
so that I might hear the breathing of God,
or tamed my heartbeat with an exercise,
or starved for visions.
Although I have watched him often
I have not become the heron,
leaving my body on the shore,
and I have not become the luminous trout,
leaving my body in the air.

I have not worshipped wounds and relics,
or combs of iron,
or bodies wrapped and burnt in scrolls.

I have not been unhappy for ten thousand years.
During the day I laugh and during the night I sleep.
My favourite cooks prepare my meals,
my body cleans and repairs itself,
and all my work goes well.

You Have the Lovers

You have the lovers,
they are nameless, their histories only for each other,
and you have the room, the bed and the windows.
Pretend it is a ritual.
Unfurl the bed, bury the lovers, blacken the windows,

let them live in that house for a generation or two.
No one dares disturb them.
Visitors in the corridor tip-toe past the long closed door,
they listen for sounds, for a moan, for a song:
nothing is heard, not even breathing.
You know they are not dead,
you can feel the presence of their intense love.
Your children grow up, they leave you,
they have become soldiers and riders.
Your mate dies after a life of service.
Who knows you? Who remembers you?
But in your house a ritual is in progress:
it is not finished: it needs more people.
One day the door is opened to the lovers' chamber.
The room has become a dense garden,
full of colours, smells, sounds you have never known.
The bed is smooth as a wafer of sunlight,
in the midst of the garden it stands alone.
In the bed the lovers, slowly and deliberately and silently,
perform the act of love.
Their eyes are closed,
as tightly as if heavy coins of flesh lay on them.
Their lips are bruised with new and old bruises.
Her hair and his beard are hopelessly tangled.
When he puts his mouth against her shoulder
she is uncertain whether her shoulder
has given or received the kiss.
All her flesh is like a mouth.
He carries his fingers along her waist
and feels his own waist caressed.
She holds him closer and his own arms tighten around her.
She kisses the hand beside her mouth.
It is his hand or her hand, it hardly matters,
there are so many more kisses.
You stand beside the bed, weeping with happiness,
you carefully peel away the sheets
from the slow-moving bodies.
Your eyes are filled with tears, you barely make out the lovers.

As you undress you sing out, and your voice is magnificent
because now you believe it is the first human voice
heard in that room.
The garments you let fall grow into vines.
You climb into bed and recover the flesh.
You close your eyes and allow them to be sewn shut.
You create an embrace and fall into it.
There is only one moment of pain or doubt
as you wonder how many multitudes are lying beside your body,
but a mouth kisses and a hand soothes the moment away.

As the Mist Leaves No Scar

[handwritten annotations:] simple, clear, beautiful
images
— sypisicn
— comes like mist — drifts off
again
— encounters in nature — moon +
sun
— life goes on
— we'll survive
— hard words — scar, hawk
— each stanza — encounter
with a different
woman?
One night stand

As the mist leaves no scar
On the dark green hill,
So my body leaves no scar
On you, nor ever will.

When wind and hawk encounter,
What remains to keep?
So you and I encounter,
Then turn, then fall to sleep.

As many nights endure
Without a moon or star,
So will we endure
When one is gone and far.

Now of Sleeping

Under her grandmother's patchwork quilt
a calico bird's-eye view
of crops and boundaries

naming dimly the districts of her body
sleeps my Annie like a perfect lady

Like ages of weightless snow
on tiny oceans filled with light
her eyelids enclose deeply
a shade tree of birthday candles
one for every morning
until the now of sleeping

The small banner of blood
kept and flown by Brother Wind
long after the pierced bird fell down
is like her red mouth
among the squalls of pillow

Bearers of evil fancy
of dark intention and corrupting fashion
who come to rend the quilt
plough the eye and ground the mouth
will contend with mighty Mother Goose
and Farmer Brown and all good stories
of invincible belief
which surround her sleep
like the golden weather of a halo

Well-wishers and her true lover
may stay to watch my Annie
sleeping like a perfect lady
under her grandmother's patchwork quilt
but they must promise to whisper
and to vanish by morning—
all but her one true lover.

The Genius

For you
I will be a ghetto jew
and dance
and put white stockings
on my twisted limbs
and poison wells
across the town

For you
I will be an apostate jew
and tell the Spanish priest
of the blood vow
in the Talmud
and where the bones
of the child are hid

For you
I will be a banker jew
and bring to ruin
a proud old hunting king
and end his line

For you
I will be a Broadway jew
and cry in theatres
for my mother
and sell bargain goods
beneath the counter

For you
I will be a doctor jew
and search
in all the garbage cans
for foreskins
to sew back again

(Handwritten annotations):

Contemporary speech / conversational tone — technique Bible

Stereotypes that
Gentiles see in Jews
- historic snapshots of Jews
- a postate Jew - denies religion.

white stockings - bikes, dress
for sabbath.
- twisted limbs - limping, sickly,
ugly
- dance - happy, dance, sing
poison wells - implies Jews do anything for himself-
revenge

killed Christ
tattle tale
betray people Judas
reveal secret rituals
Talmud - holy book
- bones of child - murdered
person Christ child
- Rothchildes - Vienna
- Shilocke ruining merchant
of Venice.

- showbiz, writers, actors
singers
cry in theatres - Jewish mama
smothers him, castrates him
pushes her son
bargain goods - rags, macys
fashion industry, furriers.

Doctor Jew professional
Jew
- circumsism.

For you
I will be a Dachau jew
and lie down in lime
with twisted limbs   *concentration*
and bloated pain   *camp.*
no mind can understand

Style

I don't believe the radio stations
of Russia and America
but I like the music and I like
the solemn European voices announcing jazz
I don't believe opium or money
though they're hard to get
and punished with long sentences
I don't believe love
in the midst of my slavery I
do not believe
I am a man sitting in a house
on a treeless Argolic island
I will forget the grass of my mother's lawn
I know I will
I will forget the old telephone number
Fitzroy seven eight two oh
I will forget my style
I will have no style
I hear a thousand miles of hungry static
and the old clear water eating rocks
I hear the bells of mules eating
I hear the flowers eating the night
under their folds
Now a rooster with a razor
plants the haemophilia gash across
the soft black sky
and now I know for certain

I will forget my style
Perhaps a mind will open in this world
perhaps a heart will catch rain
Nothing will heal and nothing will freeze
but perhaps a heart will catch rain
America will have no style
Russia will have no style
It is happening in the twenty-eighth year
of my attention
I don't know what will become
of the mules with their lady eyes
or the old clear water
or the giant rooster
The early morning greedy radio eats
the governments one by one the languages
the poppy fields one by one
Beyond the numbered band
a silence develops for every style
for the style I laboured on
an external silence like the space
between insects in a swarm
electric unremembering
and it is aimed at us
(I am sleepy and frightened)
it makes toward me brothers

For E. J. P.

I once believed a single line
        in a Chinese poem could change
                forever how blossoms fell
and that the moon itself climbed on
        the grief of concise weeping men
                to journey over cups of wine
I thought invasions were begun for crows
        to pick at a skeleton

dynasties sown and spent
to serve the language of a fine lament
    I thought governors ended their lives
        as sweetly drunken monks
telling time by rain and candles
    instructed by an insect's pilgrimage
        across the page—all this
so one might send an exile's perfect letter
to an ancient home-town friend

I chose a lonely country
    broke from love
        scorned the fraternity of war
I polished my tongue against the pumice moon
    floated my soul in cherry wine
        a perfumed barge for Lords of Memory
to languish on to drink to whisper out
    their store of strength
        as if beyond the mist along the shore
their girls their power still obeyed
    like clocks wound for a thousand years
I waited until my tongue was sore

Brown petals wind like fire around my poems
    I aimed them at the stars but
        like rainbows they were bent
before they sawed the world in half
    Who can trace the canyoned paths
        cattle have carved out of time
wandering from meadowlands to feasts
    Layer after layer of autumn leaves
        are swept away
Something forgets us perfectly

The Music Crept by Us

I would like to remind
the management
that the drinks are watered
and the hat-check girl
has syphilis
and the band is composed
of former SS monsters
However since it is
New Year's Eve
and I have lip cancer
I will place my
paper hat on my
concussion and dance

[handwritten annotations:]
Colloquial? 2nd person / 1st person
form of insanity / insanity of modern life.
- insanity of modern life.
- shallow meaningless celebration.
Hogmanay - Scottish New Year.
- shares - loner, doesn't like groups crowds quiet, thoughtful
SS monsters - Secret Police demonic images
- music - crept
- feels foolish by being there lip cancer - everything is wrong

Disguises

I am sorry that the rich man must go
and his house become a hospital.
I loved his wine, his contemptuous servants,
his ten-year-old ceremonies.
I loved his car which he wore like a snail's shell
everywhere, and I loved his wife,
the hours she put into her skin,
the milk, the lust, the industries
that served her complexion.
I loved his son who looked British
but had American ambitions
and let the word aristocrat comfort him
like a reprieve while Kennedy reigned.
I loved the rich man: I hate to see
his season ticket for the Opera
fall into a pool for opera-lovers.

I am sorry that the old worker must go
who called me mister when I was twelve
and sir when I was twenty
who studied against me in obscure socialist
clubs which met in restaurants.
I loved the machine he knew like a wife's body.
I loved his wife who trained bankers
in an underground pantry
and never wasted her ambition in ceramics.
I loved his children who debate
and come first at McGill University.
Goodbye old gold-watch winner
all your complex loyalties
must now be borne by one-faced patriots.

Goodbye dope fiends of North Eastern Lunch
circa 1948, your spoons which were not
Swedish Stainless, were the same colour
as the hoarded clasps and hooks
of discarded soiled therapeutic corsets.
I loved your puns about snow
even if they lasted the full seven-month
Montreal winter. Go write your memoirs
for the Psychedelic Review.

Goodbye sex fiends of Beaver Pond
who dreamed of being jacked-off
by electric milking machines.
You had no Canada Council.
You had to open little boys
with a pen-knife.
I loved your statement to the press:
'I didn't think he'd mind.'
Goodbye articulate monsters
Abbott and Costello have met Frankenstein.

I am sorry that the conspirators must go
the ones who scared me by showing me
a list of all the members of my family.

I loved the way they reserved judgement
about Genghis Khan. They loved me because
I told them their little beards
made them dead-ringers for Lenin.
The bombs went off in Westmount
and now they are ashamed
like a successful outspoken Schopenhauerian
whose room-mate has committed suicide.
Suddenly they are all making movies.
I have no one to buy coffee for.

I embrace the changeless:
the committed men in public wards
oblivious as Hassidim
who believe that they are someone else.
Bravo! Abelard, viva! Rockefeller,
have these buns, Napoleon,
hurrah! betrayed Duchess.
Long live you chronic self-abusers!
you monotheists!
you familiars of the Absolute
sucking at circles!
You are all my comfort
as I turn to face the beehive
as I disgrace my style
as I coarsen my nature
as I invent jokes
as I pull up my garters
as I accept responsibility.

You comfort me
incorrigible betrayers of the self
as I salute fashion
and bring my mind
        like a promiscuous air-hostess
handing out parachutes in a nose dive
bring my butchered mind
to bear upon the facts.

Two Went to Sleep

Two went to sleep
almost every night
one dreamed of mud
one dreamed of Asia
visiting a zeppelin
visiting Nijinsky
Two went to sleep
one dreamed of ribs
one dreamed of senators
Two went to sleep
two travellers
The long marriage
in the dark
The sleep was old
the travellers were old
one dreamed of oranges
one dreamed of Carthage
Two friends asleep
years locked in travel
Good night my darling
as the dreams waved goodbye
one travelled lightly
one walked through water
visiting a chess game
visiting a booth
always returning
to wait out the day
One carried matches
one climbed a beehive
one sold an earphone
one shot a German
Two went to sleep
every sleep went together
wandering away
from an operating table
one dreamed of grass

one dreamed of spokes
one bargained nicely
one was a snowman
one counted medicine
one tasted pencils
one was a child
one was a traitor
visiting heavy industry
visiting the family
Two went to sleep
none could foretell
one went with baskets
one took a ledger
one night happy
one night in terror
Love could not bind them
Fear could not either
they went unconnected
they never knew where
always returning
to wait out the day
parting with kissing
parting with yawns
visiting Death till
they wore out their welcome
visiting Death till
the right disguise worked

1964

God Is Alive

From *Beautiful Losers*

God is alive. Magic is afoot. God is alive. Magic is afoot. God is afoot. Magic is alive. Alive is afoot. Magic never died. God never sickened. Many poor men lied. Many sick men lied. Magic never weakened. Magic never hid. Magic always ruled. God is afoot. God never died. God was ruler though his funeral lengthened. Though his mourners thickened Magic never fled. Though his shrouds were hoisted the naked God did live. Though his words were twisted the naked Magic thrived. Though his death was published round and round the world the heart did not believe. Many hurt men wondered. Many struck men bled. Magic never faltered. Magic always led. Many stones were rolled but God would not lie down. Many wild men lied. Many fat men listened. Though they offered stones Magic still was fed. Though they locked their coffers God was always served. Magic is afoot. God rules. Alive is afoot. Alive is in command. Many weak men hungered. Many strong men thrived. Though they boasted solitude God was at their side. Nor the dreamer in his cell, nor the captain on the hill. Magic is alive. Though his death was pardoned round and round the world the heart would not believe. Though laws were carved in marble they could not shelter men. Though altars built in parliaments they could not order men. Police arrested Magic and Magic went with them for Magic loves the hungry. But Magic would not tarry. It moves from arm to arm. It would not stay with them. Magic is afoot. It cannot come to harm. It rests in an empty palm. It spawns in an empty mind. But Magic is no instrument. Magic is the end. Many men drove Magic but Magic stayed behind. Many strong men lied. They only passed through Magic and out the other side. Many weak men lied. They came to God in secret and though they left him nourished they would not tell who healed. Though mountains danced before them they said that God was dead. Though his shrouds were hoisted the naked God did live. This I mean to whisper to my mind. This I mean to laugh with in my mind. This I mean my mind to serve till service is but Magic moving through the world, and mind itself is Magic coursing through the flesh, and flesh itself is Magic dancing on a clock, and time itself the Magic Length of God.

<u>Theme</u> — <u>major</u> — ~~Stress~~ = the wear and tear on our
bodies (physically, emotionally +
psychologically)

i) Escape - ~~take off~~, leave, runaway, suicide

ii) Confrontation - fight it out.

iii) ~~Adaption~~ Adaptation - laugh at it, keeping cool, don't worry
about it, who cares.

Marion chose to take iii) adaptation to cope with her
stress.

- <u>Marion and her stress.</u>
- single life to → married life.
- her job, no future, dead-end job, she is to shy to work with
the public.
- lady downstairs.
- Anxiety
- bathroom + stairs   - no control over her life.

D.G. Jones

Portrait of Anne Hébert

The sunlight, here and there,
Touches a table

And a draught at the window
Announces your presence,

You take your place in the room
Without fuss,

Your delicate bones,
Your frock,
Have the grace of disinterested passion.

Words are arrayed
Like surgical instruments
Neatly in trays.

Deftly, you make an incision
Probing
The obscure disease.

Canadian illusions [handwritten]

i) small town girl leave's for big city. allusions - better job, good career, exciting job, own place /apartement, except the parents, looking for a good man (lawyer, doctor etc) [handwritten]

D. G. JONES

Your sensibility
Has the sure fingers of the blind:

Each decision
Cuts like a scalpel
Through tangled emotion.

ii) Education - BA. no good today. [handwritten]

iii) advertising + consumption as an indication of a high standart of living / a quality of life. [handwritten]

You define
The morbid tissue, laying it bare

iv) marriage + motherhood. - big step, not ready. [handwritten]

Like a tatter of lace
Dark
On the paper.

v) the carefree bachelor. [handwritten]

Little Night Journey

I

After the sun like a wound
has flared across the evening sky
inflaming the roofs of houses,
the blind panes, the faces
                of late children
halting by the river reflecting its last cry—
night descends.
                The sounds of the earth,
                mouse, bittern,
                wind sifting the grass,
turn like keys on the lost self,
shattered by light,
by whine, clash, chattering day's wake . . .
                Now factories,
cranes, timbers, dead shapes,
dramatize the dark; blundering hulks
                choked in their whistles
stand, absurd villains in black,

spilling—shavings and refuse—
silver to the cloudy moon.
The acts, encounters, items accomplished
                    lie like lumber on the shore,
scattered
and wooden as my body under the effortless stars.

II

                At the touch, at the sound
                of wind, of the water
                light on the delicate shore,
awakening like Lazarus from the fitful dream
(the excrement of that dream become
boards, clean earth, rusted iron,
thick and floating in the floating moon
and riding to the night bird's song)
                I behold
                the boatman with his wooden pole
glide in the shadows of the passing moon,
where the sandbar mirrors its ghost
and the sleeping spirits of the sleeping town,
invisible, move on the impulse of his quiet wrist . . .
                behold,
                in an acre of reeds,
as again in the gentle disturbance
the fisherman glides, my soul in his eyes,
                marshes, wing-spanned,
                reaches of foam,
and over the rolling surf of the bushes
grasslands that climb
to mountains bending currents to the stars.

III

                In the cloud of the calm, birds
                rustle, flatter the air
                with sudden escape
till their wings lie down, and frogs

winnow the stillness with voices, and down
in the veined, hyaline darkness
fish wind—primitive rhythms,
shimmering, black, under the threshold of sound.
                    The nightwind over the river
wakening marshes
freshens the thwarts with the smell of the stars.
                    The fisherman knows
                    the claws, demanding,
                    fluid toils, the breath expiring,
heard, the breath ecstatic strike like rain,
like tears. Upon such calm
                    the pole's stroke,
                    the slightest note,
leaf in the current of the blood,
slides
like the fisherman's boat, like a moon,
into the deep waters of the open heart.

IV

                    So in moods of cloud
                    while wind-swaying tufts of grass
                    measure the hours
the fisherman soul, naked, glides
through the arteries of night, on the heart's beat,
by meadow and marsh, white barn,
woodlands owl-watched, clearing where deer
drink by the shore: all pastoral lands,
                    all thickets and hollows
                    where the blood curls warm—
and then, again, past lanterns, by frenetic tracks,
wires, the shadow-hung, towering eaves of the town
whose networked arms, rigid and strong,
hang like gibbets, waiting for the black morn.

Odysseus

A Monologue in the Underworld

When last did the sun
Arm with brightness all my arms, and lie
In the folds of my black sail?
Where are the bright salt waves?
And the salt flesh of the wave-born girls?

In this distance of memory they fade.
Even the image of the spoiled
City, smouldering on the morning sky,
Grows insubstantial as a shade.
Styx and Lethe, black, flow through the mind.

.What cities, and men, what girls
Might have known this face, these eyes,
What faces might my eyes have known,
Since, discarding faces, lives,
I fled across the waters red with suns
In search of one face, life, and home?

About the pit of sacrifice, the fires
Like tongues thirsting for sound
Flare, and flicker on the brain.
Surrounded by the voiceless shades
Whose throats are eager for this blood, I bare
The sword of my refusal to their baleful eyes.

When will the blind man come? When
With this blood—O great communion—
May I give these shadows tongue? And sail
Outward, homeward, to a land of men?
Old Shadow! from these shadows, come.

I am blind. Aiee, I am struck blind!
All those faces—all, are mine!
World upon world unfolds, salt with foam,

Or tears, with love's salt hair: cities and men,
Girls, arms and oarlocks, all the cattle of the sun.

They are gathered in the fold
Of my dark sail; they are folded in the sun.
The sun engulfs the restless sea. Not a cloud
Appears. Endless and shining, beyond all
Pillars of Hercules, lovely and tempestuous,
The ocean rolls, and rolls.

My sight returns, and darkness—
Palpable with shadows crowding to the blood;
Shadows which now speak to me of homely things
And then depart, like figures in a dream.
My men—I hear them shouting down the wind.
Oh, once again, I smell the grey, salt sea.

Beautiful Creatures Brief as These

FOR JAY MACPHERSON

Like butterflies but lately come
From long cocoons of summer
These little girls start back to school
To swarm the sidewalks, playing-fields,
And litter air with colour.

So slight they look within their clothes,
Their dresses looser than the Sulphur's wings,
It seems that even if the wind alone
Were not to break them in the lofty trees,
They could not bear the weight of *things*.

And yet they cry into the morning air
And hang from railings upside down
And laugh, as though the world were theirs
And all its buildings, trees, and stones
Were toys, were gifts of a benignant sun.

For Françoise Adnet

It is that time of day, time
To chop the beans, to peel
Potatoes for the evening meal.

The fullness of time
Grows, at this hour,
Like the shadows on the crockery.

Mademoiselle's mauve gloves,
Alone, tell of the afternoon, the dried
Flowers, the delicate hands among the stalks.

For once things are what they are,
Until my little girl
Comes in from outdoors, the melting snow

Cool in her nostrils,
Sky, blue without clouds,
Behind her eyes.

But even these dissolve.
Fingering an orange
She lets her bare legs dangle.

Time is space, it glows
Like the white tablecloth,
The breadboard where I slice the onions.

The kitchen floats in my tears—
And the sun
In its brazier of urban trees.

These Trees Are No Forest of Mourners

They had dragged for hours.
The weather was like his body,
Cold, though May. It rained.

It had rained for three days—
In the grass, in the new leaves,
In the black boughs against the sky.

The earth oozed,
Like the bottom of the lake—
Like a swamp. They stared

At the drowned grass, at the leaves
That dripped in the water—aware
Of their own death, heavy

As the black boughs of the spruce
Moving in a current under the grey
Surface of the sky—aware

Of a supreme ugliness, which seemed
In its very indifference,
Somehow, to defy them:

The sodden body of the world
And of their only son.

Let them be. Oh hear me,

Though it cannot help you. They exist
Beyond your grief; they have their own
Quiet reality.

Summer Is a Poem by Ovid

FOR MICHAEL ONDAATJE

The fire falls, the night
Grows more profound.
The music is composed
Of clear chords
And silence. We become
Clear and simple as the forms
Of music; we are dumb
As water
Mirroring the stars.

Then summer is
Ovidian, and every sun
Is but a moth evolving
In the large gloom,
An excerpt from
Ars Amoris: flame
Is no more fleeting than the limbs
Of boy and girl: the conflagration
Is the same.

While the fire falls, and night
Grows more profound, the flesh,
The music and the flame
All undergo
Metamorphosis. The sounds
Of music make a close,
So with our several selves,
Together, until silence shall compose
All but the ashes in the pale dawn
And even those.

I Thought There Were Limits

I thought there were limits, Newtonian
Laws of emotion—

I thought there were limits to this falling away,
This emptiness. I was wrong.

The apples, falling, never hit the ground.

So much for grass, and animals—
Nothing remains,
No sure foundation on the rock. The cat

Drifts, or simply dissolves.

L'homme moyen sensuel
Had better look out: complete
Deprivation brings

Dreams, hallucinations which reveal
The sound and fury of machines
Working on nothing—which explains

God's creation: *ex nihilo fecit.*

Wrong again. I now suspect
The limit is the sea itself,
The limitless.

So, neither swim nor float. Relax.
The void is not so bleak.

Conclude: desire is but an ache,
An absence. It creates
A dream of limits

And it grows in gravity as that takes shape.

On a Picture of Your House

The first pale shoots
the plants make flower
into the picture of your house:

full summer reigns
there in the silence where the sun
showers cataracts of light,

shuts out all other sound.

Only in extremes like that
can I protect you, touch—
as lately, in your presence,

I could not. Only
after you'd gone, fallen,
the street so steep and dark,

could I look after you.

As spring is here
never so intense
as at the end of winter with the ice

still breathing off the lake,

so I attend you in that house
consumed by light,
that garden to which flowers

point, and which is not,

no place. And I confess
what I protect is your
capacity for loss,

your freedom to be no one, look
so naked from that window
you are lost in light.

Beyond the Photograph

The abandoned
settler's cabin is above
in the cool wind, the sun

combing the hill and the wild
apple trees.

The children, sisters of the road,
pose a moment, arm in arm
and seated

on the white crown.

The woods seem empty but for leaves.

The road
goes toward encounter, casual,
portentous (for who knows

where this road goes
in time?)

The sky might be a keyhole in the trees.

You, who know
the ragged ditches and the paved
highway—gardens ruined, the wires

singing in the wind
in cities, know

no man knows where this road goes

nor summer's
serpent in the leaves.

Nocturne: In the Way of a Love Song

Walls are not vanquished by darkness,
        it is light
        makes them merely façades,

But the plash of a fountain echoes
From the old stones. The pavement
Breathes, and a garden
Breathes like a sleeper beyond it.

            The lilies have closed,
But the water still sways in the dark,
In the gaze (stone eyes in the darkness)
Of the blind god.

For sight has turned back on its roots
        to find eyes in the ramparts,
        antennae in stone:

The thief with his hands on the dresser,
The lovers
With their mouths in their hands—

Night leaves the sleepers exposed,
        and the unlit lamp by the bedside,
        and a girl

            turning the cards in the shadow
            of a brown shade—

And the murderer knows
That the thing which he lugs to the cellar
     cannot be hidden.
                      Thunder
     east of the city, the wind
     shakes the light in the leaves.

     The dead are about us,
Caesar unburied, and the voice of a mob
Growing fainter. It fades.

     The construction pots gutter.

     Tomorrow, tomorrow, tomorrow:

In the anarchist laughter, in the grave
Voices of gamblers, the taunts
Of a young tough—in the wake

Of the penitent's prayer, in the path
Of the sailing cathedral.
Beyond the low cloud, the drift of the clover,
More loud
Than the roar of the powerhouse,

Tomorrow prepares

     all that there is—

     with the lightning of cockcrow
     all that there was.

And the lilies shall open their eyes
     in the glitter of sunlight.

Tomorrow. But now,
In the rush of the wind, in the dark,
    when the surface is shaken,

       when the mirror is shaken,
       and towers, stars,
       all are a tremble of blossom,

The roots
Are threading the darkness,

The fountain grows louder,

       and wherever you are in the rain
       and the gaunt spaces,
       asleep, or in trouble,

I am always your lover: walls

       and the fences of time,
       or the night, but discover
       the world has been joined

       indivisible, everywhere, ever.

I stand on the cobbles and listen
To the multitudinous voices.

In the silence of wind, in the endless
City of silence,   we are together.

The Stream Exposed With All Its Stones

The stream exposed with all its stones
Flung on a raw field
Is covered, once again,

With snow.

It is not hidden. It
Still flows.

The houses in the valley, standing
Motionless below,
Seem wrapped in sunlight like a snow

And are deceptive. Even stones
Deceive us.

The creator goes
Rampaging through our lives: winter
Is a masquerade.

I tell you
Nakedness is a disguise: the white
Is dark below.

This silence is the water's cry.

I tell you in those silent houses girls
Are dancing like the stones.

GREGORY COOK

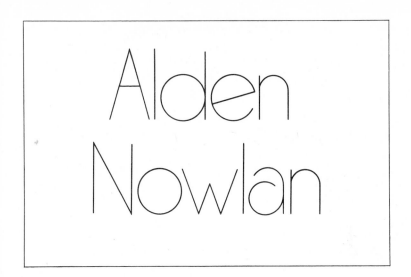

Beginning

From that they found most lovely, most abhorred,
my parents made me: I was born like sound
stroked from the fiddle to become the ward
of tunes played on the bear-trap and the hound.

Not one, but seven entrances they gave
each to the other, and he laid her down
the way the sun comes out. Oh, they were brave,
and then like looters in a burning town.

Their mouths left bruises, starting with the kiss
and ending with the proverb, where they stayed;
never in making was there brighter bliss,
followed by darker shame. Thus I was made.

Warren Pryor

When every pencil meant a sacrifice
his parents boarded him at school in town,
slaving to free him from the stony fields,
the meagre acreage that bore them down.

They blushed with pride when, at his graduation,
they watched him picking up the slender scroll,
his passport from the years of brutal toil
and lonely patience in a barren hole.

When he went in the Bank their cups ran over.
They marvelled how he wore a milk-white shirt
work days and jeans on Sundays. He was saved
from their thistle-strewn farm and its red dirt.

And he said nothing. Hard and serious
like a young bear inside his teller's cage,
his axe-hewn hands upon the paper bills
aching with empty strength and throttled rage.

God Sour the Milk of the Knacking Wench

God sour the milk of the knacking wench
with razor and twine she comes
to stanchion our blond and bucking bull,
pluck out his lovely plumbs.

God shiver the prunes on her bark of chest,
who capons the prancing young.
Let maggots befoul her alive in bed,
and dibble thorns in her tongue.

For Nicholas of All the Russias

Wind in a rocky country and the harvest
meagre, the sparrows eaten, all the cattle
gone with the ragged troopers, winter coming,
mother will starve for love of you and wrapping
newest and least accustomed leave him squalling
out in the hills beside the skulls of foxes,
it cold and snow in the air. Stranger, knocking,
(now in this latter time even the poor
have bread and sleep on straw) what silly rumour
tells me your eyes are yellow and your lips
once rose trout-quick to suck a she-wolf's teats?

Our Lord, his peaked heir and hawk-faced daughters
are gone, although they say one severed finger
was found after the soldiers cleaned the cellar.

I, Icarus

There was a time when I could fly. I swear it.
Perhaps, if I think hard for a moment, I can even tell you
      the year.
My room was on the ground floor at the rear of the house.
My bed faced a window.
Night after night I lay on my bed and willed myself to fly.
It was hard work, I can tell you.
Sometimes I lay perfectly still for an hour before I felt
      my body rising from the bed.
I rose slowly, slowly until I floated three or four feet
      above the floor.
Then, with a kind of swimming motion, I propelled myself
      toward the window.

Outside, I rose higher and higher, above the pasture fence,
    above the clothesline, above the dark, haunted trees
    beyond the pasture.
And, all the time, I heard the music of flutes.
It seemed the wind made this music.
And sometimes there were voices singing.

And He Wept Aloud, So That the Egyptians Heard It

In my grandfather's house
for the first time in years,
houseflies big as bumblebees
playing crazy football
in the skim-milk-coloured windows,

leap-frogging from
the cracked butter saucer
to our tin plates of
rainbow trout and potatoes, catching the bread
on its way to our mouths,
    mounting one another
    on the rough deal table.

It was not so much their filth
as their numbers and persistence and—
oh, admit this, man, there's no point in poetry
if you withhold the truth
once you've come by it—
    their symbolism:
    Baal-Zebub,
god of the poor and outcast,

that enraged me, made me snatch the old man's
Family Herald, attack them like a maniac,
lay to left and right until the window sills

over-flowed with their smashed corpses,
until bits of their wings
stuck to my fingers,
until the room buzzed with their terror . . .

And my grandfather, bewildered and afraid,
came to help me:
    'never seen a year
    when the flies were so thick'
as though he'd seen them at all before I came!

His voice so old and baffled and pitiful
that I threw my club into the wood box and sat down
    and wanted to beg his forgiveness
as we ate on in silence broken only
by the almost inaudible humming
of the flies rebuilding their world.

Britain Street

Saint John, New Brunswick

This is a street at war.
The smallest children
battle with clubs
till the blood comes,
shout 'fuck you!'
like a rallying cry—

while mothers shriek
from doorsteps and windows
as though the very names
of their young were curses:

'Brian! Marlene!
Damn you! God damn you!'

or waddle into the street
to beat their own with switches:
'I'll teach you, Brian!
I'll teach you, God damn you!'

On this street,
even the dogs
would rather fight
than eat.

I have lived here nine months
and in all that time
have never once heard
a gentle word spoken.

I like to tell myself
that is only because
gentle words are whispered
and harsh words shouted.

In Those Old Wars

In those old wars
where generals wore yellow ringlets
and sucked lemons at their prayers,
other things being equal
the lost causes were the best.

Lee rode out of history
on his gray horse, Traveller,
so perfect a hero
had he not existed
it would have been necessary to invent him—
war stinks without gallantry.

An aide, one of the few who survived,
told him,
Country be damned, general,
for six months these men
have had no country but you.
They fought barefoot
and drank blueberryleaf tea.

The politicians
strung up Grant
like a carrot,
made him a Merovingian.
They stole everything,
even the coppers from Lincoln's dead eyes.

In those days, the vanquished
surrendered their swords like gentlemen,
the victors alone
surrendered their illusions.
The easiest thing to do for a Cause
is to die for it.

July 15

The wind is cool. Nothing is happening.
I do not strive for meaning. When I lie on my back
the wind passes over me, I do not feel it.
The sun has hands
like a woman, calling the heat
out of my body.
The trees sing. Nothing is happening.

When I close my eyes,
I hear the soft footsteps
of the grass. Nothing is happening.

How long have I lain here?
Well, it is still summer. But is it the same
summer I came?
I must remember
not to ask myself questions.
I am naked. Trees sing. The grass walks.
Nothing is happening.

The Mysterious Naked Man

A mysterious naked man has been reported
on Cranston Avenue. The police are performing
the usual ceremonies with coloured lights and sirens.
Almost everyone is outdoors and strangers are conversing
    excitedly
as they do during disasters when their involvement is
    peripheral.
'What did he look like?' the lieutenant is asking.
'I don't know,' says the witness. 'He was naked.'
There is talk of dogs—this is no ordinary case
of indecent exposure, the man has been seen
a dozen times since the milkman spotted him and now
the sky is turning purple and voices
carry a long way and the children
have gone a little crazy as they often do at dusk
and cars are arriving
from other sections of the city.
And the mysterious naked man
is kneeling behind a garbage can or lying on his belly
in somebody's garden
or maybe even hiding in the branches of a tree,
where the wind from the harbour
whips at his naked body,
and by now he's probably done
whatever it was he wanted to do
and wishes he could go to sleep
or die
or take to the air like Superman.

Another Parting

Is this what it's like to be old?
To have endured so many partings
that this time I scarcely feel
the throat's tensing for the blow,
the sick pendulum in the belly,

feel only my pain
flowing into
an all-encompassing sadness

like the sound of that high plane,
full of people I don't know,
people I can hardly imagine,

breaking the silence
of this dark room
where I lie sleepless.

For Claudine Because I Love Her

Love is also
my finding this house
emptier than a stranger
ever could.

Is it the sound of your movements
enlivening the chairs
although I hear nothing, is it the weight
of your small body moving the house
so little no machine
could ever assess it,
though my mind knows,
is it some old
wholly animal instinct

that fills every room with you,
gently, so I am aware of it only

when I come home
and there is nothing here.

Ypres: 1915

The age of trumpets is passed, the banners hang
like dead crows, tattered and black,
rotting into nothingness on cathedral walls.
In the crypt of St Paul's I had all the wrong thoughts,
wondered if there was anything left of Nelson
or Wellington, and even wished
I could pry open their tombs and look,
then was ashamed
of such morbid childishness, and almost afraid.

I know the picture is as much a forgery
as the Protocols of Zion, yet it outdistances
more plausible fictions: newsreels, regimental histories,
biographies of Earl Haig.
                        It is always morning
and the sky somehow manages to be red
though the picture is in black and white.
There is a long road over flat country,
shell holes, the debris of houses,
a gun carriage overturned in a field,
the bodies of men and horses,
but only a few of them and those
always neat and distant.
                        The Moors are running
down the right side of the road.
The Moors are running
in their baggy pants and Santa Claus caps.
The Moors are running.
                        And their officers,

Frenchmen who remember
Alsace and Lorraine,
are running backwards in front of them,
waving their swords, trying to drive them back,
weeping
      at the dishonour of it all.
The Moors are running.

And on the left side of the same road,
the Canadians are marching
in the opposite direction.

The Canadians are marching
in English uniforms behind
a piper playing 'Scotland the Brave'.

The Canadians are marching
in impeccable formation,
every man in step.

The Canadians are marching.

And I know this belongs
with Lord Kitchener's mustache
and old movies in which the Kaiser and his general staff
seem to run like the Keystone Cops.

That old man on television last night,
a farmer or fisherman by the sound of him,
revisiting Vimy Ridge, and they asked him
what it was like, and he said,
There was water up to our middles, yes
and there was rats, and yes
there was water up to our middles
and rats, all right enough,
and to tell you the truth
after the first three or four days
I started to get a little disgusted.

Oh, I know they were mercenaries
in a war that hardly concerned us.
I know all that.

Sometimes I'm not even sure that I have a country.

But I know they stood there at Ypres
the first time the Germans used gas,
that they were almost the only troops
in that section of the front
who did not break and run,
who held the line.

Perhaps they were too scared to run.
Perhaps they didn't know any better
—that is possible, they were so innocent,
those farmboys and mechanics, you have only to look
at old pictures and see how they smiled.
Perhaps they were too shy
to walk out on anybody, even Death.
Perhaps their only motivation
was a stubborn disinclination.

Private MacNally thinking:
You squareheaded sons of bitches,
you want this God damn trench
you're going to have to take it away
from Billy MacNally
of the South End of Saint John, New Brunswick.

And that's ridiculous, too, and nothing
on which to found a country.
                              Still
It makes me feel good, knowing
that in some obscure, conclusive way
they were connected with me
and me with them.

The First Stirring of the Beasts

The first stirring of the beasts
is heard at two or three or four
in the morning, depending on the season.

You lie, warm and drowsy, listening,
wondering how there is so much difference
between the sounds
cattle and horses make,
moving in their stanchions or halters,
so much difference that you can't explain,
so that if someone asked you
which of them is moving now?
you couldn't answer
but lying there, not quite awake,
you know, although it doesn't matter,
and then a rooster crows
and it sounds, or maybe you imagine this,
unsure and a little afraid,
                                    and after a little
there are only the sounds of night
that we call silence.

The second stirring of the beasts
is the one everybody understands.
You hear it at dawn
and if you belong here
you get up.
Anyway, there is no mystery
in it, it is the other stirring,
the first brief restlessness
which seems to come for no reason
that makes you ask yourself
what are they awake for?

Margaret Avison

Snow

Nobody stuffs the world in at your eyes.
The optic heart must venture: a jail-break
And re-creation. Sedges and wild rice
Chase rivery pewter. The astonished cinders quake
With rhizomes. All ways through the electric air
Trundle candy-bright disks; they are desolate
Toys if the soul's gates seal, and cannot bear,
Must shudder under, creation's unseen freight.
But soft, there is snow's legend: colour of mourning
Along the yellow Yangtze where the wheel
Spins an indifferent stasis that's death's warning.
Asters of tumbled quietness reveal
Their petals. Suffering this starry blur
The rest may ring your change, sad listener.

The World Still Needs

Frivolity is out of season.
Yet, in this poetry, let it be admitted
The world still needs piano-tuners
And has fewer, and more of these
Gray fellows prone to liquor
On an unlikely Tuesday, gritty with wind,
When somewhere, behind windows,
A housewife stays for him until the
      Hour of the uneasy bridge-club cocktails
      And the office rush at the groceteria
      And the vesper-bell and lit-up buses passing
      And the supper trays along the hospital corridor,
Suffering from
Sore throat and dusty curtains.

Not all alone on the deserted boathouse
Or even on the prairie freight
(The engineer leaned out, watchful and blank
And had no Christmas worries
Mainly because it was the eve of April),
Is like the moment
When the piano in the concert-hall
Finds texture absolute, a single solitude
For those hundreds in rows, half out of overcoats,
Their eyes swimming with sleep.

From this communal cramp of understanding
Springs up suburbia, where every man would build
A clapboard in a well of Russian forest
With yard enough for a high clothesline strung
To a small balcony . . .
A woman whose eyes shine like evening's star
Takes in the freshblown linen
While sky a lonely wash of pink is still
Reflected in brown mud
Where lettuces will grow, another spring.

New Year's Poem

The Christmas twigs crispen and needles rattle
Along the windowledge.
         A solitary pearl
Shed from the necklace spilled at last week's party
Lies in the suety, snow-luminous plainness
Of morning, on the windowledge beside them.
And all the furniture that circled stately
And hospitable when these rooms were brimmed
With perfumes, furs, and black-and-silver
Crisscross of seasonal conversation, lapses
Into its previous largeness.
         I remember
Anne's rose-sweet gravity, and the stiff grave
Where cold so little can contain;
I mark the queer delightful skull and crossbones
Starlings and sparrows left, taking the crust,
And the long loop of winter wind
Smoothing its arc from dark Arcturus down
To the bricked corner of the drifted courtyard,
And the still windowledge.
         Gentle and just pleasure
It is, being human, to have won from space
This unchill, habitable interior
Which mirrors quietly the light
Of the snow, and the new year.

To Professor X, Year Y

The square for civic receptions
Is jammed, static, black with people in topcoats
Although November
Is mean, and day grows late.

The newspapermen, who couldn't
Force their way home, after the council meeting
&c., move between windows and pressroom
In ugly humour. They do not know
What everybody is waiting for
At this hour
To stand massed and unmoving
When there should be—well—nothing to expect
Except the usual hubbub
Of city five o'clock.

Winter pigeons walk the cement ledges
Urbane, discriminating.

Down in the silent crowd few can see anything.
It is disgusting, this uniformity
Of stature.
If only someone climbed in pyramid
As circus families can . . .
Strictly, each knows
Downtown buildings block all view anyway
Except, to tease them,
Four narrow passages, and ah
One clear towards open water
(If 'clear'
Suits with the prune and mottled plumes of
Madam night).

Nobody gapes skyward
Although the notion of
Commerce by air is utterly
familiar.

Many citizens at this hour
Are of course miles away, under
Rumpus-room lamps, dining-room chandeliers,
Or bound elsewhere.
One girl who waits in a lit drugstore doorway

North 48 blocks for the next bus
Carries a history, an ethics, a Russian grammar,
And a pair of gym shoes.

But the few thousand inexplicably here
Generate funny currents, zigzag
Across the leaden miles, and all suburbia
Suffers, uneasily.

You, historian, looking back at us,
Do you think I'm not trying to be helpful?
If I fabricated cause-and-effect
You'd listen? I've been dead too long for fancies.
Ignore us, hunched in these dark streets
If in a minute now the explosive
Meaning fails to disperse us and provide resonance
Appropriate to your chronicle.

But if you do, I have a hunch
You've missed a portent.
('Twenty of six.' 'Snow?—I wouldn't wonder.')

The Swimmer's Moment

For everyone
The swimmer's moment at the whirlpool comes,
But many at that moment will not say
'This is the whirlpool, then.'
By their refusal they are saved
From the black pit, and also from contesting
The deadly rapids, and emerging in
The mysterious, and more ample, further waters.
And so their bland-blank faces turn and turn
Pale and forever on the rim of suction
They will not recognize.
Of those who dare the knowledge

Many are whirled into the ominous centre
That, gaping vertical, seals up
For them an eternal boon of privacy,
So that we turn away from their defeat
With a despair, not for their deaths, but for
Ourselves, who cannot penetrate their secret
Nor even guess at the anonymous breadth
Where one or two have won:
(The silver reaches of the estuary).

Voluptuaries and Others

That Eureka of Archimedes out of his bath
Is the kind of story that kills what it conveys;
Yet the banality is right for that story, since it is not a
    communicable one
But just a particular instance of
The kind of lighting up of the terrain
That leaves aside the whole terrain, really,
But signalizes, and compels, an advance in it.
Such an advance through a be-it-what-it-may but take-it-not-
    quite-as-given locale:
Probably that is the core of being alive.
The speculation is not a concession
To limited imaginations. Neither is it
A constrained voiding of the quality of immanent death.
Such near values cannot be measured in values ·
Just because the measuring
Consists in that other kind of lighting up
That shows the terrain comprehended, as also its containing
    space,
And wipes out adjectives, and all shadows
        (or, perhaps, all but shadows).

The Russians made a movie of a dog's head
Kept alive by blood controlled by physics, chemistry, equip-
    ment, and

Russian women scientists in cotton gowns with writing tablets.
The heart lay on a slab midway in the apparatus
And went phluff, phluff.
Like the first kind of illumination, that successful experiment
Can not be assessed either as conquest or as defeat.
But it is living, creating the chasm of creation,
Contriving to cast only man to brood in it, further.

History makes the spontaneous jubilation at such moments
    less and less likely though,
And that story about Archimedes does get into public school
    textbooks.

Birth Day

Saturday I ran to Mitilene.

Bushes and glass along the grass-still way
Were all dabbled with rain
And the road reeled with shattered skies.

Towards noon an inky, petulant wind
Ravelled the pools, and rinsed the black grass round them.

Gulls were up in the late afternoon
And the air gleamed and billowed
And broadcast flung astringent spray
                                All swordy-silver.
I saw the hills lie brown and vast and passive.

The men of Mitilene waited restive
Until the yellow melt of sun.
I shouted out my news as I sped towards them
That all, rejoicing, could go down to dark.

All nests, with all moist downy young
Blinking and gulping daylight; and all lambs

Four-braced in straw, shivering and mild;
And the first blood-root up from the ravaged beaches
Of the old equinox; and frangible robins' blue
Teethed right around to sun:
These first we loudly hymned;
And then
The hour of genesis
When first the moody firmament
Swam out of Arctic chaos,
Orbed solidly as the huge frame for this
Cramped little swaddled creature's coming forth
To slowly, foolishly, marvellously
Discover a unique estate, held wrapt
Away from all men else, which to embrace
Our world would have to stretch and swell with strangeness.

This made us smile, and laugh at last. There was
Rejoicing all night long in Mitilene.

Pace

'Plump raindrops in these
faintly clicking groves,
the pedestrians' place, July's
violet and albumen
close?'

'No. No. It is perhaps the conversational side-effect
among the pigeons; behold
the path-dust is nutmeg powdered and
bird-foot embroidered.'

> The silk-fringed hideaway
> permits the beechnut-cracking
> squirrels to plumply
> pick and click and
> not listen.

Pedestrians linger
striped stippled sunfloating
    at the rim of the
          thin-wearing groves

letting the ear experience this
discrete, delicate
clicking.

Black-White Under Green:
May 18, 1965

This day of the leafing-out
speaks with blue power—
among the buttery grassblades
white, tiny-spraying spokes on the end of a weed-stem
and in the formal beds, tulips
and invisible birds inaudibly hallooing,
enormous, their beaks out wide, throats bulging, aflutter,
eyes weeping with speed
where the ultraviolets play and the scythe of the jets
flashes, carrying
the mind-wounded heartpale person, still a boy, a pianist, dying
        not
of the mind's wounds (as they read the x-rays) but
dying, fibres separated, parents ruddy and
American, strong, sheathed in the cold of
years of his differentness, clustered by two at
the nether arc of his flight.

This day of the leafing-out is one to remember
    how the ice crackled among
      stiff twigs. Glittering strongly
        the old trees sagged. Boughs
    abruptly unsocketed. Dry, orange gashes
the dawn's fine snowing discovered and powdered over.

. . . to remember the leaves ripped loose
the thudding of the dark sky-beams
and the pillared plunging sea
shelterless. Down the centuries
a flinching speck
        in the white fury found of itself—and another—
the rich blood spilling, mother to child, threading
the perilous combers, marbling
the surges, flung
out, and ten-fingered, feeling for
the lollop, the fine-wired
music, dying skyhigh
still between carpets and the
cabin-pressuring windows
on the day of the leafing.

Faces fanned by
rubberized, cool air
are opened; eyes wisely
smile.
The tulips, weeds, new leaves
neither smile nor are scorning to smile nor uncertain,
dwelling in light.
A flick of ice, fire, flood,
far off from
the day of the leafing-out I knew
when knee-wagon small, or from my
father's once at a horse-tail silk-shiny
fence-corner or this
day when the runways wait
white in the sun, and a new leaf is
metal, torn out of that blue
afloat in the dayshine.

July Man

Old, rain-wrinkled, time-soiled, city-wise, morning man
whose weeping is for the dust of the elm-flowers
and the hurting motes of time,
rotted with rotting grape,
sweet with the fumes,
puzzled for good by fermented potato-
peel out of the vat of the times,
turned out and left
in this grass-patch, this city-gardener's place
under the buzzing populace's
square shadows, and the green shadows
of elm and ginkgo and lime
(planted for Sunday strollers and summer evening
families, and for those
bird-cranks with bread-crumbs
and crumpled umbrellas who come
while the dew is wet on the park, and beauty
is fan-tailed, gray and dove gray, aslant, folding in
from the white fury of day).

In the sound of the fountain
you rest, at the cinder-rim, on your bench.

The rushing river of cars
makes you a stillness, a pivot, a heart-stopping
blurt, in the sorrow
of the last rubbydub swig, the searing, and
stone-jar solitude lost, and yet,
and still—wonder (for good now) and
trembling:

> The too much none of us knows
> is weight, sudden sunlight, falling
> on your hands and arms, in your lap,
> all, all, in time.

The Absorbed

The sun has not absorbed
this icy day, and this day's industry—in
behind glass—hasn't the blue and gold, cold
outside. Though not absorbing, this
sought that:

> sheeted, steely, vaulted,
> all gleam, this morning;
> bright blue with one stained wing in the
>   northeast, at lunch hour;
> in early afternoon
> abruptly a dust-flurry,
>   all but this private coign of place
>   deafened, all winding in one cloth of moth.
> Then space breathed, hollowing twilight
>   on ice and the pale-gray, pale-blue,
>   and far fur-colored wooden trees
>   and ornamental trees.

Towards sundown
a boy came with an aluminum toboggan.
He worked his way, absorbed,
past footmark pocks, on crust,
up ice-ridge, sometimes bumping
down to the Japanese yews, sometimes
scooter-shoving athwart the hill,
then, with a stake,
kneeling,
he paddles, thrusting, speed-wise, then
stabbing, uphill; then
dangling the rope and poring on
slope-sheen, standing, he stashes
the aluminum, upright, in a frost-lumpy shoal
and beside coasting motorcars and parked cars
listens . . . and off again, toque to the eyebrows,
alone still in the engulfing dark.

The inside breathing here
closes down all the window but a visor-slit
on the night glare.
                    New cold is
in dry-thorn nostrils.

Alone, he plays, still there. We
struggle, our animal fires
pitted against those
several grape-white stars,
their silence.

In a Season of Unemployment

These green painted park benches are
all new. The Park Commissioner had them
planted.
Sparrows go on
having dust baths at the edge of
the park maple's shadow, just where
the bench is cemented down, planted
and then cemented.

   Not a breath moves
   this newspaper.
   I'd rather read it by the Lapland sun at midnight. Here we're
   bricked in early by a
   stifling dark.

On that bench a man in a
pencil-striped white shirt
keeps his head up and steady.

   The newspaper-astronaut says
   'I feel excellent under the condition of weightlessness.'
And from his bench a

scatter of black bands in the hollow-air
ray out—too quick for the eye—
and cease.

    'Ground observers watching him on a TV circuit said
    At the time of this report he
    was smiling,' Moscow ra-
    dio reported.
I glance across at him, and mark that
he is feeling
excellent too, I guess, and
weightless and
'smiling'.

A Nameless One

Hot in June a narrow winged
long-elbowed-thread-legged
living insect lived
and died within
the lodgers' second-floor bathroom here.

At six a.m.
wafting ceilingward,
no breeze but what it living made there;

at noon standing
still as a constellation of spruce needles
before the moment of
making it, whirling;

at four a
wilted flotsam, cornsilk, on the linoleum:

now that it is
over, I
look with new eyes
upon this room
adequate for one to
be, in.

Its insect-day
has threaded a needle
for me for my eyes dimming
over rips and tears and
thin places.

A Castle and Two Inhabitants

I

The several stories of the castle,
Placed rickety like box on box
Or like those Chinese puzzles
That are whole outside but inside
Piece in piece, were carpentered
A while ago. The builder is inside.
We think he must be, for we never
Saw him leave it, nor indeed go in.

It simply stands there, stands,
Though how it stands no one explains,
Nor how to go from room to room,
Nor why the king has chosen it
Upon a dreadful plane of space
To live in, there to hold his court.

II

There is a hunchback in the court
Who loves his daughter and who serves
The king with stories of a hunchback love.
The crooked ways are best, he says,
The only way a cripple learns to move,
And love is crooked and the twist is this:
My hunchback proves it.

                  Like the sun at noon
Hunched over earth that splendid hump
Curls round his body, like a swollen pear
Hung from a leafless tree, like the earth
On Atlas as he sways beneath its load.
He lumps it in our faces and he leers
About our daughters and he loves his own
And monthly serves the king a wreath,
The queen's own hair upon a horn.

III

There is a wizard also in our court
Who is both man and woman and who knows
How women love, who says the hunchback
Lied to us. Love is triangular, he cries,
And shining algebras fall from his cap
Made out of crystals shivered from a frost
Of passion.
           Sculpt from a crust of sky
An ice-cold man is propped on snowy stalks
Of dogma, double-eyed with embered coals.

Here generation ends. This simple love,
The wizard says, endures the rollick
Lust and summer of a hunchback sun.

Acis

There was her message. Suddenly
His blood had turned to water.
She looked into his eyes and saw
They swam, no shore behind them,
Looking toward the green and lighted sea,
A fish-like stare, a dolphin memory.

Pillar of Fire

A man came to my tent door
in the heat of the day, the tent
stretched and slapped in the wind.
All the guy ropes went taut
And I felt my temples stretch
and throb in the noise and heat.

He talked about blowflies,
plague among the swollen cattle.
He asked about the children.
'You are a great nation.
Will you stay here long?'

That night the fire in the tent
vomited a great smoke.
The tent glowed like a furnace.
I dreamt about Egypt and its flies,
a priest dying of cancer.
I am told to breed more children,
try not to think about politics,
remember the Sabbath and my enemies.

Thief Hanging in Baptist Halls

After a Sculpture by George Wallace

Amid the congratulations of summer,
polite vegetation, deans, a presbyterian sun,
brick minds quaintly shaped in gothic and glass,
here where the poise and thrust of speech
gleams like polished teak
I did not expect to see myself.

But there he hangs
shrugging on his hung lines,
soft as a pulped fruit or bird
in his welded soft suit of steel.

I wish he would not shrug
and smile weakly at me
as if ashamed that he is hanging there,
his dean's suit fallen off, his leg cocked
as if to run
or (too weak, too tired, too undone)
to do what can be done
about his nakedness.

Why should he hang there,
my insulting self, my deanship, all undone?

He dangles while the city bursts in green and steel,
black flower in the mouth of my speech:
the proud halls reel,
gothic and steel melt in the spinning sun.

The Meaning of the I CHING

I

unopened
           book of old men
           orange-blossom book
                                     before me
you were
           how could you contain me?

do you not see I am the mouths
of telegraphs and cemeteries?
my mother groaned like the whole
of Western Union to deliver
my message
                     and yelling birthdays
that unrolled from my lungs
like ticker-tape for presidents
about to be murdered
                                I sped
on a line that flew
to the vanishing point of the west

before I was
                     you were
unopened book
                     do not craze me
with the odour of orange-blossom

do not sit there
like smiling old men

           how could you contain me?

II

under my fingers words form themselves
it's crazy to talk of temples in this day
but light brightens on my page
like today moving against the wooden house
all shapes change and yet stay
as if they were marble in autumn
as if in the marbled yellow autumn
each western house becomes a shrine
stiff against the age of days
under my fingers stiffly formed

one cannot be another, I cry,
let me not be crazed by poetry

I will walk in streets that vanish
noting peculiar elms like old women
who will crash under the storm of sun
that breaks elm, woman, man
into a crumble of stump and bark
until the air is once more clear
in the sane emptiness of fall

III

my body speaks to me
as my arms say: two are one
as my feet say: earth upon earth
as my knees say: bow down, unhinge yourself
as my cells say: we repeat the unrepeatable

the book speaks: arrange yourself in the form
                       that will arrange you

before I was: colours that hurt me
                       arranged themselves in me

before I was: horizons that blind me
                       arranged themselves in me

before I was: the dead who speak to me
                       arranged themselves in me

IV

I am the mouths
of smiling old men

there rises from me
the scent of orange-blossoms

I speak in the words
of the ancient dead

arranged
in the raging sun
in the stiffening age of days

and in the temple of my house

one becomes another
I am crazed by poetry

Houdini

I suspect he knew that trunks are metaphors,
could distinguish between the finest rhythms
unrolled on rope or singing in a chain
and knew the metrics of the deepest pools

I think of him listening to the words
spoken by manacles, cells, handcuffs,
chests, hampers, roll-top desks, vaults,
especially the deep words spoken by coffins

escape, escape: quaint Harry in his suit
his chains, his desk, attached to all attachments
how he'd sweat in that precise struggle
with those binding words, wrapped around him
like that mannered style, his formal suit

and spoken when? by whom? What thing first said
'there's no way out'?; so that he'd free himself,
leap, squirm, no matter how, to chain himself again,
once more jump out of the deep alive
with all his chains singing around his feet
like the bound crowds who sigh, who sigh.

Pictures in an Institution

I

Notice: all mirrors will be covered
           the mailman is forbidden to speak
           professors are confined to their offices
           faculties no longer exist.

II

I speak of what I know,
how uncle Asher, spittle on his lips,
first typed with harvest hands the fox
across a fence and showing all good men
come to their country's aid rushed off to Israel
there to brutalize his wife and son

how step-grandfather Barak wiped
sour curds out of his curly beard
before he roared the Sabbath in my ears
what Sara, long his widow, dreamed

the night she cried: God, let him die at last,
thinking perhaps of Josef who had lost
jewels in Russia where the Cossack rode
but coughed his stomach out in Winnipeg

Your boredom does not matter. I take,
brutal to my thoughts, these lives, defy
your taste in metaphor; the wind-break
on the farm that Barak plowed to dust
makes images would ruin public poetry.

The rites of love I knew:
how father cheated brother, uncle, son,
and bankrupt-grocer, that we might eat
wrote doggerel verse, later took his wife,
my mother, in the English way beside my bed.
Why would he put his Jewishness aside?
Because there was no bread?
                              Or out of spite
that doctors sliced his double rupture,
fingered spleen, and healed his bowel's ache?

Lovers lie down in glades, are glad.
These, now in graves, their headstones sunk,
knew nothing of such marvels, only God, his ways,
owning no texts of Greek or anthropology.

III

Notice: the library is closed to all who read
          any student carrying a gun
          registers first, exempt from fines,
          is given thirteen books per month,
          one course in science, one in math,
          two options
                      campus police
          will see to co-eds' underwear

IV

These names I rehearse:
                    Eva, Isaac,
Charley, Yetta, Max
                    now dead
or dying or beyond my lies

till I reeling with messages
and sick to hold again their bitter lives
put them, with shame, into my poetry.

V

Notice: there will be no further communication
          lectures are cancelled
          all students are expelled
          the reading of poetry is declared a public
                                              crime

Woodbine

When a crooked man meets beauty
You think there'd be shouting in the streets

I wish there were no allegories
I wish the doctors could do something about my forked tongue

Believe me, I have gone about with pails on my head
so that my friends would recognize me.

Lord, Lord, pollution everywhere
But I breathe still
                    and breathless, sweet
woodbine, colour of honey, touches my skin
as if my unbelieving eyes made no difference at all

The Speaking Earth

grandfathers fall into it
their mighty beards muffled in grass

and admirals, the sea-sounding men

lovers fall into the earth
like rain on wet dark bodies

listen, our lady earth flowers
into the sea-green language
of grass and drowned admirals

listen: in bearded branches
clasped like broken hands
admiring birds
lovers singing of their kiss
before and after all the words

From the North Saskatchewan

when on the high bluff discovering
the river cuts below
                          send messages
we have spoken to those on the boats

I am obsessed by the berries they eat
all night odour of Saskatoon
and an unidentifiable odour
something baking
                     the sun
never reaches the lower bank

I cannot read the tree markings

today the sky is torn by wind:
a field after a long battle
strewn with corpses of cloud

give blessings to my children
speak for us to those who sent us here
say we did all that could be done
we have not learned
what lies north of the river
or past those hills that look like beasts

Marina

Because she spoke often of the sea we thought she had known
        another country, her people distant, not forgotten

We did not know then who was calling her or what songs she
        listened to or why the sea-birds came to rest
        upon her long fingers

Or why she would shudder like a sea-bird about to take flight,
        her eyes changing with the changing light

As the sea-changing opal changes, as a shell takes its
        colours from the sea as if it were the sea

As if the great sea itself were held in the palm of a hand

They say the daughters of the sea know the language of birds,
        that in their restless eyes the most fortunate learn
        how the moon rises and sets

We do not know who is calling her or why her eyes change
        or what shore she will set her foot upon

On the 25th Anniversary of the
Liberation of Auschwitz:
Memorial Services, Toronto, YMHA,
Bloor & Spadina, January 25, 1970

the name is hard
a German sound made out of
the gut guttural throat
y scream yell   ing   open
voice mouth growl
                    and sweat

'the only way out of Auschwitz
is through the chimneys'
                        of course
that's second hand   that's told
again   Sigmund   Sherwood   (Sobolewski)
twisting himself into that sentence
before us on the platform

                        the poem
shaping itself late in the after
noon later than it would be:

Pendericki's 'Wrath of God'
moaning electronic Polish theatric
the screen silent
                    framed by the name
looking away from/ pretending not there
no   name   no not   name   no

          Auschwitz
     in   GOTHIC   lettering
                        the hall
a parody a reminiscence a nasty memory
the Orpheum in Estevan before Buck Jones

the Capital in Regina before Tom Mix
waiting for the guns
waiting for the cowboy killers
one two three
            Legionnaires
Polish ex-prisoners Association
Legions
            their medals their flags

so the procession, the poem gradually
insistent beginning to shape itself
with the others
                walked with them
into the YMHA Bloor & Spadina
thinking apocalypse shame degradation
thinking bones and bodies melting
thickening thinning melting bones and bodies
thinking not mine/ speak clearly
the poet's words/ Yevtyshenko at Baba-Yar

there   this January   snow
heavy wet   the wind   heavy wet
the street grey white slush melted concrete
bones and bodies melting slush
                              saw
with the others
                the prisoner
in the YMHA hall Bloor & Spadina
arms wax stiff body stiff unnatural
coloured face blank eyes
                        walked
with the others toward the screen
toward the pictures
                SLIDES

        this is mother
        this is father
        this is
                the one who is

waving her arms like that
is the one who
                    like
I mean running with her breasts bound
ing
        running
                    with her hands here and there
with her here and
                        there
hands
        that   that is

the poem becoming the body
becoming the faint hunger
ing body
            prowling
                        through
words the words words the words
opening   mouths   ovens
the generals smiling saluting
in their mythic uniforms god-like
generals uniforms with the black leather
with the straps and intricate leather
the phylacteries the prayer shawl
corsets and the boots and the leather straps
and the shining faces of the generals in their boots
and their stiff wax bodies their unnatural faces
and their blank eyes and their hands their stiff hands
and the generals in their straps and wax and stiff
staying standing
                    melting bodies and thickening
                    quick flesh on flesh handling
                    hands

        the poem flickers, fades
the four Yarzeit candles guttering   one
        each four million lights dim
my words drift
                    smoke from chimneys and ovens

a bad picture, the power failing
pianist clattering on and over and through
the long Saturday afternoon in the Orpheum
while the whitehatted star spangled cowboys
shot the dark men and shot the dark men
and we threw popcorn balls and grabbed
each other and cheered:

me jewboy yelling
for the shot town and the falling men
and the lights come on
and

with the others
standing in silence

the gothic word hangs
over us on a shroud-white screen

and we drift away
to ourselves
to the late Sunday *Times*

the wet snow
the city

a body melting

- Totem - people - people like totems - totems
like people.

II words - become pebbles - hard round useless
also like birds - flying away

III animals take shape of hard & vise versa
- talking about a relationship - Margaret Atwood &
guy
- relationship is out
- stanley park - Vancouver
- relationship is dying
- nothing at all to worship - especially each
other - people not smiling
        - wooden people
        - uprooted transplanted
        - pleasant on the outside
        - totem is still part of life cycle -
        created - lived - died - decayed - back
                to earth

Three sections formed around - exchange - transposition (handwritten)

Margaret Atwood

Image of loss of contemporary experience (handwritten)

shared image (handwritten)

experience (handwritten)

there are few totems that remain living for us (handwritten)
- dead relationship (handwritten)
- dead trees, sacred meadows, dead roots, not much (handwritten)
  fun talking was difficult - had nothing to say (handwritten)
  when did - words heavy - meaningless - just (handwritten)
  conversation to cut monotony (handwritten)

Some Objects of Wood and Stone

I. TOTEMS

doll hard (handwritten)
fright - three level transposition - word - (handwritten)
pebbles (handwritten)

We went to the park
where they kept the wooden people:
static, multiple
uprooted and trans-
planted.

- birds - pebbles - words fly (handwritten)
- carved animals - stone (handwritten)
- person grows cold too (handwritten)
- other persons cold (handwritten)

Their faces were restored,
freshly-painted.
In front of them
the other wooden people
posed for each other's cameras
and nearby a new booth
sold replicas and souvenirs.

- hard unfeeling - human being (handwritten)
- image of in our shape (handwritten)

concrete object to show human experience (handwritten)

One of the people was real.
It lay on its back, smashed

by a toppling fall or just
the enduring of minor winters.
Only one of the heads had
survived intact, and it was
also beginning to decay
but there was a
life in the progressing
of old wood back to
the earth, obliteration

that the clear-hewn
standing figures lacked.

As for us, perennial watchers,
tourists of another kind
there is nothing for us to worship;
no pictures of ourselves, no blue-
sky summer fetishes, no postcards
we can either buy, or
smiling
be.

There are few totems that remain
living for us.
Though in passing,
through glass we notice

dead trees in the seared meadows
dead roots bleaching in the swamps.

II. PEBBLES

Talking was difficult. Instead
we gathered coloured pebbles
from the places on the beach
where they occurred.

They were sea-smoothed, sea-completed.
They enclosed what they intended
to mean in shapes
as random and necessary
as the shapes of words

and when finally
we spoke
the sounds of our voices fell
into the air   single and
solid and rounded and really
there
and then dulled, and then like sounds
gone,   a fistful of gathered
pebbles there was no point
in taking home, dropped on a beachful
of other coloured pebbles

and when we turned to go
a flock of small
birds flew scattered by the
fright of our sudden moving
and disappeared: hard

sea pebbles
thrown solid for an instant
against the sky

flight of words

III. CARVED ANIMALS

The small carved
animal is passed from
hand to hand
around the circle
until the stone grows warm

touching, the hands do not know
the form of animal
which was made or
the true form of stone
uncovered

and the hands, the fingers the
hidden small bones
of the hands bend to hold the shape,
shape themselves, grow
cold with the stone's cold, grow
also animal, exchange
until the skin wonders
if stone is human

In the darkness later
and even when the animal
has gone, they keep
the image of that
inner shape

hands holding warm
hands holding
the half-formed air

The Islands

There are two of them:

One larger, with steep granite
cliffs facing us, dropping sheer
to the deep lake;

the other smaller, closer
to land, with a reef running
out from it and dead trees
grey, waist-high in the water.

We know they are alone
and always will be.

The lake takes care of that
and if it went,
they would be hills
and still demand
separateness
from the eye.

Yet, standing on the cliff
(the two
of us)
on our bigger island,
looking,

we find it pleasing
(it soothes our instinct for
symmetry, proportion,
for company perhaps)

that there are two of them.

The Animals in That Country

In that country the animals
have the faces of people:

the ceremonial
cats possessing the streets

the fox run
politely to earth, the huntsmen
standing around him, fixed
in their tapestry of manners

the bull, embroidered
with blood and given
an elegant death, trumpets, his name
stamped on him, heraldic brand
because

(when he rolled
on the sand, sword in his heart, the teeth
in his blue mouth were human)

he is really a man

even the wolves, holding resonant   — *Germany*
conversations in their
forests thickened with legend.

> In this country the animals
> have the faces of
> animals.

> Their eyes
> flash once in car headlights
> and are gone.

> Their deaths are not elegant.

> They have the faces of
> no-one.

A Night in the Royal Ontario Museum

Who locked me

into this crazed man-made
stone brain
                    where the weathered

totempole jabs a blunt
finger at the byzantine
mosaic dome

Under that ornate
golden cranium I wander
among fragments of gods, tarnished
coins, embalmed gestures
chronologically arranged,
looking for the EXIT sign

but in spite of the diagrams
at every corner, labelled
in red: YOU ARE HERE
the labyrinth holds me,

turning me around
the cafeteria, the washrooms,
a spiral through marble
Greece and Rome, the bronze
horses of China

then past the carved masks, wood and fur
to where 5 plaster Indians
in a glass case
squat near a dusty fire

and further, confronting me
with a skeleton child, preserved
in the desert air, curled
beside a clay pot and a few beads.

I say I am far
enough,   stop here   please
no more

but the perverse museum, corridor
by corridor, an idiot

voice jogged by a pushed
button, repeats its memories

and I am dragged to the mind's
deadend, the roar of the bone-
yard, I am lost
among the mastodons
and beyond: a fossil
shell, then

samples of rocks
and minerals, even the thundering
tusks dwindling to pin-
points in the stellar
fluorescent-lighted
wastes of geology

Progressive Insanities of a Pioneer

*Lack of order – foils
Pioneer from Europe
– land out of order – is defeated
– atwood – Canadian all losers
– struggle for survival*

I

He stood, a point
on a sheet of green paper
proclaiming himself the centre,

victim figure
1st guard branch theme alienation
of modern man "The seren..."

*psycological & emotional)
hazards of a pioneer
anguish of spirit
–each of 7 parts – a picture
or phase*

with no walls, no borders
anywhere; the sky no height
above him, totally un-
enclosed

*– sees himself as centre of
universe
– sharp images – tearing things & nives
& hooks
– no walls, no borders – totally
enclosed*

and shouted:

*2nd
attempt at order – rows
regular lines
I am not
random
part of
plan*

Let me out!

*– spacial concepts – prison, corners
open, borderless – idea – personality
trickles out. fear of
out doors*

II

He dug the soil in rows,
imposed himself with shovels.

*chorist?
statements of troth
–nature talks back with its own troth – keep sprouting up again
– stubborness talking – understood land
–harmlessweed, doesn't impose order and conflict that
–attempt to impose begins with land & reality*

He asserted
into the furrows, I
am not random.

The ground
replied with aphorisms:

a tree-sprout, a nameless
weed, words
he couldn't understand.

III

The house pitched
the plot staked
in the middle of nowhere.

At night the mind
inside, in the middle
of nowhere.

The idea of an animal
patters across the roof.

In the darkness the fields
defend themselves with fences
in vain:
        everything
        is getting in.

IV

By daylight he resisted.
He said, disgusted
with the swamp's clamourings and the outbursts
of rocks,
        This is not order
        but the absence
        of order.

He was wrong, the unanswering
forest implied:

> It was
> an ordered absence

v

For many years
he fished for a great vision,
dangling the hooks of sown
roots under the surface
of the shallow earth.

It was like
enticing whales with a bent
pin. Besides he thought

in that country
only the worms were biting.

VI

If he had known unstructured
space is a deluge
and stocked his log house-
boat with all the animals

even the wolves,

he might have floated.

But obstinate he
stated, The land is solid
and stamped,

watching his foot sink
down through stone
up to the knee.

VII

Things
refused to name themselves; refused
to let him name them.

The wolves hunted
outside.

On his beaches, his clearings,
by the surf of under-
growth breaking
at his feet, he foresaw
disintegration
                and in the end
through eyes
made ragged by his
effort, the tension
between subject and object,

the green
vision, the unnamed
whale invaded.

*complete triumph
of wilderness
man has lost
Battle.*

Further Arrivals

After we had crossed the long illness
that was the ocean, we sailed up-river

On the first island
the immigrants threw off their clothes
and danced like sandflies

We left behind one by one
the cities rotting with cholera,
one by one our civilized
distinctions

and entered a large darkness.

It was our own
ignorance we entered.

I have not come out yet

My brain gropes nervous
tentacles in the night, sends out
fears hairy as bears,
demands lamps; or waiting

for my shadowy husband, hears
malice in the trees' whispers.

I need wolf's eyes to see
the truth.

I refuse to look in a mirror.

Whether the wilderness is
real or not
depends on who lives there.

Death of a Young Son by Drowning

He, who navigated with success
the dangerous river of his own birth
once more set forth

on a voyage of discovery
into the land I floated on
but could not touch to claim.

His feet slid on the bank,
the currents took him;
he swirled with ice and trees in the swollen water

and plunged into distant regions,
his head a bathysphere;
through his eyes' thin glass bubbles

he looked out, reckless adventurer
on a landscape stranger than Uranus
we have all been to and some remember.

There was an accident; the air locked,
he was hung in the river like a heart.
They retrieved the swamped body,

cairn of my plans and future charts,
with poles and hooks
from among the nudging logs.

It was spring, the sun kept shining, the new grass
lept to solidity;
my hands glistened with details.

After the long trip I was tired of waves.
My foot hit rock. The dreamed sails
collapsed, ragged.

> I planted him in this country
> like a flag.

The Immigrants

They are allowed to inherit
the sidewalks involved as palmlines, bricks
exhausted and soft, the deep
lawnsmells, orchards whorled
to the land's contours, the inflected weather

only to be told they are too poor
to keep it up, or someone

has noticed and wants to kill them; or the towns
pass laws which declare them obsolete.

2nd – difficulties –
cut to a

I see them coming
up from the hold smelling of vomit, *– looked down upon –*
infested, emaciated, their skins grey *became poor*
with travel; as they step on shore

3rd – diseases

the old countries recede, become *4th – shore* *– is recede*
perfect, thumbnail castles preserved *– memories*
like gallstones in a glass bottle, the *– era of perfection*
towns dwindle upon the hillsides *5th – pitiful, few*
in a light paperweight-clear. *belongings*

6th – obstacles
– not enough money
They carry their carpetbags and trunks *– crops dry*
with clothes, dishes, the family pictures; *– drought.*
they think they will make an order
like the old one, sow miniature orchards, *7th – different*
carve children and flocks out of wood *at home*
: illusions break

but always they are too poor, the sky *8th – sees them*
is flat, the green fruit shrivels *– Canadian Map –*
in the prairie sun, wood is for burning; *always pink*
and if they go back, the towns *Europeans – sing*
– beards shawls
in time have crumbled, their tongues *– features – hidden*
stumble among awkward teeth, their ears
are filled with the sound of breaking glass.
I wish I could forget them
and so forget myself:

my mind is a wide pink map
across which move year after year
arrows and dotted lines, further and further,
people in railway cars

their heads stuck out of the windows
at stations, drinking milk or singing,
their features hidden with beards or shawls
day and night riding across an ocean of unknown
land to an unknown land.

Game After Supper

This is before electricity,
it is when there were porches.

On the sagging porch an old man
is rocking. The porch is wooden,

the house is wooden and grey;
in the living room which smells of
smoke and mildew, soon
the woman will light the kerosene lamp.

There is a barn but I am not in the barn;
there is an orchard too, gone bad,
its apples like soft cork
but I am not there either.

I am hiding in the long grass
with my two dead cousins,
the membrane grown already
across their throats.

We hear crickets and our own hearts
close to our ears;
though we giggle, we are afraid.

From the shadows around
the corner of the house
a tall man is coming to find us:

He will be an uncle,
if we are lucky.

Procedures for Underground

(Northwest Coast)

The country beneath
the earth has a green sun
and the rivers flow backwards;

the trees and rocks are the same
as they are here, but shifted.
Those who live there are always hungry;

from them you can learn
wisdom and great power,
if you can descend and return safely.

You must look for tunnels, animal
burrows or the cave in the sea
guarded by the stone man;

when you are down you will find
those who were once your friends
but they will be changed and dangerous.

Resist them, be careful
never to eat their food.
Afterwards, if you live, you will be able

to see them when they prowl as winds,
as thin sounds in our village. You will
tell us their names, what they want, who

has made them angry by forgetting them.
For this gift, as for all gifts, you must
suffer: those from the underland

will be always with you, whispering their
complaints, beckoning you
back down; while among us here

you will walk wrapped in an invisible
cloak. Few will seek your help
with love, none without fear.

Younger Sister, Going Swimming

(Northern Quebec)

Beside this lake
where there are no other people

my sister in bathing suit continues
her short desolate
parade to the end of the dock;

against the boards
her feet make sad statements
she thinks no one can hear;

(I sit in a deckchair
not counting, invisible;
the sun wavers on
this page as on a pool.)

She moves the raft out
past the sandy point;
no one comes by in a motorboat.

She would like to fill the lake
with other swimmers, with answers.
She calls her name. The sun encloses
rocks, trees, her feet in the water, the circling
bays and hills as before.

She poises, raises her arms
as though signalling, then disappears.
The lake heals itself quietly
of the wound left by the diver.
The air quakes and is still.

(Under my hand the paper
closes over these
marks I am making on it.

The words ripple, subside,
move outwards toward the shore.)

Gwendolyn MacEwen

Poems in Braille

I

all your hands are verbs,
now you touch worlds and feel their names—
thru the thing to the name
not the other way thru (in winter
I am Midas, I name gold)

the chair and table and book
extend from your fingers;
all your movements
command these things back to their
places; a fight against familiarity
makes me resume my distance

II

they knew what it meant,
those egyptian scribes who drew

eyes right into their hieroglyphs,
you read them dispassionate until
the eye stumbles upon itself
blinking back from the papyrus

outside, the articulate wind
annotates this; I read carefully
lest I go blind in both eyes, reading with
that other eye the final hieroglyph

III

the shortest distance between 2 points
on a revolving circumference
is a curved line; O let me follow you,
Wenceslas

IV

with legs and arms I make alphabets
like in those children's books
where people bend into letters and signs,
yet I do not read the long cabbala of my bones
truthfully; I need only to move
to alter the design

V

I name all things in my room
and they rehearse their names,
gather in groups, form tesseracts,
discussing their names among themselves

I will not say the cast is less than the print
I will not say the curve is longer than the line,
I should read all things like braille in this season
with my fingers I should read them
lest I go blind in both eyes reading with
that other eye the final hieroglyph

You Cannot Do This

you cannot do this to them, these are my people;
I am not speaking of poetry, I am not speaking of art.
you cannot do this to them, these are my people.
you cannot hack away the horizon in front of their eyes.

the tomb, articulate, will record your doing,
I will record it also, this is not art,
this is a kind of science, a kind of hobby,
a kind of personal vice like coin collecting.

it has something to do with horses
and signet rings and school trophies,
it has something to do with the pride of the loins,
it has something to do with good food and music,
and something to do with power, and dancing.
you cannot do this to them, these are my people.

Green With Sleep

Green with sleep the skin breathes night
—I hear you turning worlds in your dark dream—
The sheets like leaves in a private season
Speak of the singular self which lies between.

Your breathing is a thing I cannot enter
Like a season more remote than winter;
Green with sleep breathes, breathes the skin,
I hear you turning worlds in your dark dream.

There is a great unspeakable wheel which keeps
Us slender as myths, and green with sleep.

Manzini: Escape Artist

now there are no bonds except the flesh; listen—
there was this boy, Manzini, stubborn with
gut stood with black tights and a turquoise
leaf across his sex

and smirking while the big
brute tied his neck arms legs, Manzini
naked waist up and white with sweat

struggled. Silent, delinquent, he
was suddenly all teeth and knee, straining slack
and excellent with sweat, inwardly

wondering if Houdini would take as long
as he; fighting time and the drenched
muscular ropes, as though his tendons were worn
on the outside—

as though his own guts were the ropes
encircling him; it was beautiful; it was thursday; listen—
there was this boy, Manzini

finally free, slid as snake from
his own sweet agonized skin, to throw his entrails
white upon the floor
with a cry of victory—

now there are no bonds except the flesh,
but listen, it was thursday, there was this boy,
Manzini—

Arcanum One

and in the morning the king loved you most
and wrote your name with a sun and a beetle

and a crooked ankh, and in the morning
you wore gold mainly, and the king adorned you
with many more names

beside fountains, both of you slender
as women, circled and walked together
like bracelets circling water, both of you
slender as women, wrote your names with
beetles and with suns, and spoke together
in the golden mornings

and the king entered your body
into the bracelet of his name
and you became a living syllable
in his golden script, and your body
escaped from me like founting water
all the daylong

but in the evenings you wrote my name
with a beetle and a moon, and lay upon me
like a long broken necklace which had fallen
from my throat, and the king loved you
most in the morning, and his glamorous love
lay lengthwise along us all the evening

The Red Bird You Wait For

You are waiting for someone to confirm it,
You are waiting for someone to say it plain,
Now we are here and because we are short of time
I will say it; I might even speak its name.

It is moving above me, it is burning my heart out,
I have felt it crash through my flesh,
I have spoken to it in a foreign tongue,
I have stroked its neck in the night like a wish.

Its name is the name you have buried in your blood,
Its shape is a gorgeous cast-off velvet cape,
Its eyes are the eyes of your most forbidden lover
And its claws, I tell you its claws are gloved in fire.

You are waiting to hear its name spoken,
You have asked me a thousand times to speak it,
You who have hidden it, cast it off, killed it,
Loved it to death and sung your songs over it.

The red bird you wait for falls with giant wings—
A velvet cape whose royal colour calls us kings
Is the form it takes as, uninvited, it descends,
It is the Power and the Glory forever, Amen.

The Discovery

do not imagine that the exploration
ends, that she has yielded all her mystery
or that the map you hold
cancels further discovery

I tell you her uncovering takes years,
takes centuries, and when you find her naked
look again,
admit there is something else you cannot name,
a veil, a coating just above the flesh
which you cannot remove by your mere wish

when you see the land naked, look again
(burn your maps, that is not what I mean),
I mean the moment when it seems most plain
is the moment when you must begin again

Inside the Great Pyramid

all day the narrow shaft
received us; everyone
came out sweating and
gasping for air, and one
old man collapsed
upon a stair;
                    I thought:
the fact that it has stood
so long
is no guarantee
it will stand today,
but went in anyway
and heard when I was
halfway up a long
low rumbling like
the echo of ancient stones
first straining to their place;
                    I thought:
we have made this, we
have made *this*.
I scrambled out into
the scandalous sun and saw
the desert was an hourglass
we had forgotten to invert,
a tasselled camel falling
to his knees, the River
filling the great waterclock
of earth.

Cairo, 1966

One Arab Flute

1

I was innocent as a postcard
among the dark robes and bazaars;
my exiled smile shone under
the stern judicial sun;
            I drank Turkish coffee
            in the divided city
with a singular lack of irony
over the sunken tomb of Herod's family
with lovenotes scribbled on the wall
            (O really, this was also
            a British bomb shelter? Well
            well . . .)
and saw the tomb of Akiva
who was stripped by the iron
combs of Rome, and Maimonides'
cold white cone with candles
at the bottom and the top,
            and a place called Lifta
where the mouths of houses ate
the sunset, a blue-eyed Arab
with a wild profile, standing
in front of blond stone, the
blue-eyed sky over Jerusalem,
            an old artist Ephraim
            with platefuls of grapes
            and large gaudy studio
in Safed, who was very angry
and painted noisily daily and nightly
on the mystic hills,
            a Maccabean tomb for a man
            called Yason, carved
            with caramel deers.
And my camera eye,
the curious film, the tourist
lens, followed
the old stones skyward.

II

The kites, the coloured kites of Jaffa
were insolent in the sky;
        an old dead sweet smell
        and the peacock sea
        upheld them
and the parachute sun became
a pavilion and a distant throne;
I walked through pink tiles,
difficult shells, sandstone,
        and everyone asked the time
        on the beach at Jaffa
but the walls had gone down,
the walls of Jaffa,
and I saw the sea
through many naked doors;
        the kites like signals
        pointed sideways skyward
and Arab children screamed to find
bleached fish skulls like
a thousand heads of Jonah
on the shore.

III

Now through a park of palms and cocks
I come to Capernaum, reading a pamphlet
that lists Christ's miracles
like adventure serials; I pray
to the pillars standing sad
as dolmens: Hold
        the sky up forever, Amen.

Now through a park of palms and cocks
I come to Kefer-Nahum; the priest
draws a crucifix through the sweat
on my brow, and hands me
        a small grey skirt
to remind my naked western knees

that this place is holy, and I
dissolve into the scenery.

IV

Kids skip rope behind the Roman arch
in Ein Karem where the light
is graded on the terraced hills;
            there are many cats and flowers,
            bells,
and a small girl carries a loaf
of bread that reaches to her knees
and all the children come and gaze
into my camera
though some are afraid to come
too near. Behind them there's a sign
which reads: *John the Baptist*
was born here. I seem to see
in a small boy's face
a look that says:
            he who will come after me
            will bless this time, this
place.

V

The workers at Ramat Rachel
have eyes at their fingernails
and they scratch dynasties from stone;
            no one can tell them
that what they find in the itchy dirt
is more than the day's few *lira*
            (ruins of Judah's kings,
            mosaic floors)
for they *are* history, while we,
the disinherited, search here,
            scramble like the lizards
in the Byzantine church nearby,
scratch little marks all over

the holy floors, seeking
our reward.

VI

To reach Jerusalem you ride
through ribs of dead jeeps
and rusted wreaths of war
that line the road;
                you realize the City
                lives
because it was destroyed.
You sit by night close to
the barbed wire border; only
cats and spiders can pass; even
                the moon is divided here.
From Notre Dame the smashed
faces of Mary and Jesus
watch you with ugly irony;
                David's tower
is a conical hat in the moonlight;
the Mosque of Omar
has been there forever.
If I forget you, O Jerusalem,
may my right hand
build another.

VII

Noman's land is Gehenna
and leading from it the chalkwhite
salt of bleached houses, white-
faced, wide-eyed towns;
                children play
near Gehenna and they
are only playing, but I keep hearing
tofet drums beaten to dull
their screaming

as when, on the yellow grass
under
the awful shadow of Gehenna
they lay outstretched upon
the hands of Moloch
beneath his mouth of fire
and waited for the sacred knife
to spill their sweet blood over.

VIII

In Rehov Yafo
in the New Jerusalem
an Iraqi beggar I call John
        avoids curious eyes,
        watches the ground.
I see him wave away
the coins of pitying women
without even looking; the
dirty *piastres* stuffed in his fist
are enough for the day. How
solemnly he protests his station,
how
        violently he turns on them
        sometimes, cursing, his eyes
on fire; the old
American-styled suit he wears
hangs from him like a prayer.

IX

'What we must do,'
the man told me,
'Is keep them together.
That way
they are not dangerous.'
        But I have seen
        trees that grow sideways
in Esdraelon, fighting gravity;

their bark is strong
and corded with patience
and their leaves rush upwards
in incongruous dance.
        And I have seen
        bright coins worn
on foreheads, as though they told
the value of the skull
        (fill in quickly
        the arab arch, jam it
        with stones, or make
        the roundness square;
        step
        lightly through
        the eastern music)
And this—
one young Bedouin boy leading sheep
at sundown past Beersheba,
and the flute he played
was anarchy between his fingers;
I saw the poor grass move
its tender blades, I
heard the wind awakening
the desert from its sleep.

Israel 1962

Dark Pines Under Water

This land like a mirror turns you inward
And you become a forest in a furtive lake;
The dark pines of your mind reach downward,
You dream in the green of your time,
Your memory is a row of sinking pines.

Explorer, you tell yourself this is not what you came for
Although it is good here, and green;
You had meant to move with a kind of largeness,
You had planned a heavy grace, an anguished dream.

But the dark pines of your mind dip deeper
And you are sinking, sinking, sleeper
In an elementary world;
There is something down there and you want it told.

Memoirs of a Mad Cook

There's no point kidding myself any longer,
I just can't get the knack of it; I suspect
there's a secret society which meets
in dark cafeterias to pass on the art
from one member to another.
Besides,
it's so *personal* preparing food for someone's
insides, what can I possibly *know*
about someone's insides, how can I presume
to invade your blood?
I'll try, God knows I'll try
but if anyone watches me I'll *scream*
because maybe I'm handling a tomato wrong
how can I *know* if I'm handling a tomato wrong?

something is eating away at me
with splendid teeth

Wistfully I stand in my difficult kitchen
and imagine the fantastic salads and soufflés
that will never be.
Everyone seems to grow thin with me
and their eyes grow black as hunters' eyes
and search my face for sustenance.

All my friends are dying of hunger,
there is some basic dish I cannot offer,
and you my love are almost as lean
as the splendid wolf I must keep always
at my door.

- paranoid - insecure.
- not a good cook.
- she is scared the people will not like
the food she makes.
- can not give love, cold person.
all her friend feel she does not give off
enough love.

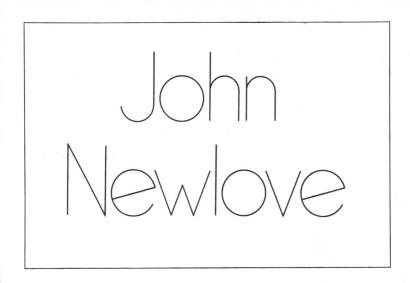

John Newlove

The Arrival

Having come slowly, hesitantly
at first, as a poem comes,
and then steadily down to the marshy sea-board—

that day I ran along a stone sea-break,
plunging into the Pacific, the sun
just setting, clothed, exuberant, hot,
so happy—
          o sing!
plunging into the ocean, rolled on my back, eyes
full of salt water, hair in eyes,
shoes lost forever at the bottom, noting
as if they were trivia
the wheeling birds of the air
and gulls gorging themselves
on the sea-going garbage

of civilization, the lower mainland,
hauled away by tugs—
                                        the gulls,
being too heavy to fly,
and foolish-looking there,
can be knocked off with sticks
from barge into ocean—

and noting the trees whitely flowering,
took off my clothes and calmly bathed.

Then, If I Cease Desiring

Then, if I cease desiring,
you may sing a song
of how young I was.

You may praise famous moments,
all have them, of the churches
I broke into for wine,

not praise, the highways
I travelled drunkenly
in winter, the cars I stole.

You may allow me moments,
not monuments, I being
content. It is little,
but it is little enough.

The Flowers

It is raining outside, rain
streaks down the window to my left,
cars sluice water in the gutters

in the night, the round
neon clock-containing sign
hanging outside beside my window
sways in the wind and buzzes.

The flowers sprout everywhere;
in pots and boxes, on lawns
and trees, in gardens and ditches,
the flowers are growing; the wet
wind will nourish them, cut
some down but feed the rest.

The sign crackles
and swings on its bar,
iron bar; the cars go by
all the night. They cut
a momentary trail and mark,
disappearing, on the wet
black pavement. The cars go by,
the police in their cars
prowl restlessly
up and down the rainy avenue,
looking for interlopers, anyone
afoot at night in the rain,
the blue and dangerous
gun-hipped cops.

The car came smashing
and wrecking his face, his head,
poor hit hurt head
bleeding on the roadway
and in the cool hospital
night in bandages
and glued-on tape.

His eyes, they said,
were soft and easy
years ago. Now,

he wears them cleverly
like some secret
coupled badge,
twin and original, dark
ice eyes that watch and assess
slowly what they have
fixed
on; his head does not move.

In the hospitals,
with antiseptic nurses
stripping him, knife-
fisted surgeons bending down,
they cut, irony,
to save his life; and he stayed
days and years filled
with tantalizing drugs, interminable
dreams, tangled in bandages and
shocks, suspicions, a nonchalant
profusion of hopes and cures,
surrounded by the tears
of his rainy crazy peers.

Rain, wind, and spring, all things
drove him crazy and grow
flowers, flowers
that dance in the rain,
the bulging flowers that grew
in his head, plants
of devil or of god, some
holy epileptic angel, bloated
inhuman flowers shining
their bright colours
insistently, turning
slowly in the wind
and spring, tortuous
creaking growths, thick
cancerous things
in the rain, stems

like the barrels of rifles,
fat lead bullet roots
gripping the damp earth.

And the cars
pass up and down
the streets, disappearing
trails, the blue police
pass, coughing delicately
behind their leathery fists,
guns dangling
from their hips, eyes
watching. My flowery clock
buzzes and mutters,
typewriter taps
like the rain. I breathe
as harshly as the wind.

Verigin, Moving in Alone,

(fatherless, 250 people,
counting dogs and gophers
we would say, Jmaeff's grocerystore,
me in grade 4, mother
principal of the 2-building,
3-room, 12-grade school,)

a boy sitting on the grass
of a small hill, the hot fall,
speaking no russian, an airgun
my sister gave me making me envied.

I tried all fall, all spring
the next ominous year, to kill
a crow with it, secretly glad
I could not, the men
in winter shooting the town's

wild dogs, casually tossing
the quick-frozen barely-bleeding
head-shot corpses onto
the street-side snowbanks,

the highway crews cutting their way
through to open the road with what
I was sure was simply
some alternate of a golden summer's
wheat-threshing machine, children
running through the hard-tossed spray,
pretending war from the monster's snout,

leaping into snowbanks from
Peter The Lordly Verigin's
palace on the edge of town
in a wild 3-dimensional
cubistic game of cops and robbers,

cold spring swimming
in Dead Horse Creek and farmers'
dugouts and doomed fishing
in beastless ponds, strapped
in school for watching a fight,

coldly holding back tears
and digging for drunken father's
rum-bottle, he had finally
arrived, how I loved him,
loved him, love him, dead, still.

My mad old brother chased me
alone in the house with him
around and around
the small living room, airgun,
rifle in hand, silently,
our breaths coming together—

all sights and temperatures
and remembrances,
as a lost gull screams now
outside my window,
a 9-year-old's year-long
night and day in tiny
magnificent prairie Verigin:

the long grey cat we got,
the bruised knees, cut fingers,
nails in feet, far walks
to watch a horse's corpse
turn slowly and sweetly to bone,
white bone, and in the late spring,
too, I remember the bright
young bodies of the boys,

my friends and peers and enemies,
till everything breaks down.

Crazy Riel

Time to write a poem
or something.
Fill up a page.
The creature noise.
Huge massed forces of men
hating each other.
What young men do not know.
To keep quiet,
contemporaneously.
Contempt. The robin diligently
on the lawn sucks up worms,
hopping from one to another.
Youthfully. Sixteen miles

from my boyhood home
the frogs sit in the grassy marsh
that looks like a golf course
by the lake. Green frogs.
Boys catch them for bait or sale.
Or caught them. Time.
To fill up a page.
To fill up a hole.
To make things feel better. Noise.
The noise of the images
that are people I will never understand.
Admire them though I may.
Poundmaker. Big Bear. Wandering Spirit,
those miserable men.
Riel. Crazy Riel. Riel hanged.
Politics must have its way.
The way of noise. To fill up.
The definitions bullets make,
and field guns.
The noise your dying makes,
to which you are the only listener.
The noise the frogs hesitate
to make as the metal hook
breaks through the skin
and slides smoothly into place
in the jaw. The noise
the fish makes caught in the jaw,
which is only an operation
of the body and the element,
which a stone would make
thrown in the same water, thrashing,
not its voice.
The lake is not displaced,
having one less jackfish body.
In the slough that looks like a golf course
the family of frogs sings. Metal throats.
The images of death hang upside-down.
Grey music.

It is only the listening for death,
fingering the paraphernalia,
the noise of the men you admire.
And cannot understand.
Knowing little enough about them.
The knowledge waxing.
The wax that paves hell's road,
slippery as the road to heaven.
So that as a man slips
he might as easily slide
into being a saint as destroyer.
In his ears the noise magnifies.
He forgets men.

Everyone

Everyone is so
lonely in this
country that
it's necessary
to be fantastic—

a crow flew over
my grave today,
no goose stepping
pompously along,

but a crow,
black as life,
raucously calling
to no one—

struggling image:
necessary
to be fantastic,
almost to lie,

but incorrect,
not cautious enough,
though not evil
actively: it does not

have the diminishing
virtue of evilness
(a locked sea-monster
with half the

dangerous coils
waving above
the grey water),
for the tourists,
glistening crows.

Lady, Lady

Lady, lady, I cannot lie,
I didn't cut down your cherry tree.

It was another man, in another season,
for the same reason.

I eat the stone and not the flesh,
it is the bare bone of desire I want,

something you would throw a dog,
or me, though I insult by saying so.

God knows it is not said
of your body, that it is like

a bone thrown to a dog,
or that I would throw it away, which

moment to moment I cannot remember
under those baggy clothes you wear—

which, if I love and tell,
I love well.

Ride Off Any Horizon

Ride off any horizon
and let the measure fall
where it may—

on the hot wheat,
on the dark yellow fields
of wild mustard, the fields

of bad farmers, on the river,
on the dirty river full
of boys and on the throbbing

powerhouse and the low dam
of cheap cement and rocks
boiling with white water,

and on the cows and their powerful
bulls, the heavy tracks
filling with liquid at the edge

of the narrow prairie
river running steadily away.

*

Ride off any horizon
and let the measure fall
where it may—

among the piles of bones
that dot the prairie

in vision and history
(the buffalo and deer,

dead indians, dead settlers
the frames of lost houses

left behind in the dust
of the depression,

dry and profound, that
will come again in the land

and in the spirit, the land
shifting and the minds

blown dry and empty—
I have not seen it! except

in pictures and talk—
but there is the fence

covered with dust, laden,
the wrecked house stupidly empty)—

here is a picture for your wallet,
of the beaten farmer and his wife
leaning toward each other—

sadly smiling, and emptied of desire.

*

Ride off any horizon
and let the measure fall
where it may—

off the edge
of the black prairie

as you thought you could fall,
a boy at sunset

not watching the sun
set but watching the black earth,

never-ending they said in school,
round: but you saw it ending,

finished, definite, precise—
visible only miles away.

*

Ride off any horizon
and let the measure fall
where it may—

on a hot night the town
is in the streets—

the boys and girls
are practising against

each other, the men
talk and eye the girls—

the women talk and
eye each other, the indians
play pool: eye on the ball.

*

Ride off any horizon
and let the measure fall
where it may—

and damn the troops, the horsemen
are wheeling in the sunshine,
the cree, practising

for their deaths: mr poundmaker,
gentle sweet mr bigbear,
it is not unfortunately

quite enough to be innocent,
it is not enough merely
not to offend—

at times to be born
is enough, to be
in the way is too much—

some colonel otter, some
major-general middleton will
get you, you—

indian. It is no good to say,
I would rather die
at once than be in that place—

though you love that land more,
you will go where they take you.

*

Ride off any horizon
and let the measure fall—

where it may;
it doesn't have to be

the prairie. It could be
the cold soul of the cities
blown empty by commerce

and desiring commerce
to fill up emptiness.

The streets are full of people.

It is night, the lights
are on; the wind

blows as far as it may. The streets
are dark and full of people.

Their eyes are fixed as far as
they can see beyond each other—

to the concrete horizon, definite,
tall against the mountains,
stopping vision visibly.

In This Reed

In this reed, in this semblance
of a human body I wear
so awkwardly, unjointed,
though I hesitate to admit,

there there is life, though
once I would have denied it, thinking
my somnolence clever evidence
of a wearied intellectuality;

but in this hunger I feed on,
in the lungs heaving and the eyes,
to speak only of the eyes
that see so little
of what they ought to see (no more
than they should!), there the life is—

it is imperfection
the eyes see, it is
impreciseness they deserve,

but they desire so much more,
what they desire, what they hope,
what they invent,

is perfection, organizing
all things as they may not be,
it is what they strive for

unwillingly, against themselves,
to see a perfect order, ordained
reason—

and what they strive against
while they wish it, what they want
to see, closed, is what
they want, and will not be.

The Engine and the Sea

The locomotive in the city's distance, obscure, misplaced,
sounds a child's horn on the flat land leading to the
cliff of dark buildings,

the foghorns on the water's edge cry back.

Between the sounds men sit in their houses watching
machines inform them in Edison's light. In the marshes,
the music of ominous living. . . .

a leggy insect runs on that surface, frogs wait, fish,
angling birds.

In the cities men wait to be told. They sit between the
locomotive and the fish. The flat sea and the prairie
that was a sea contain them. Images float before their
eyes,

men and women acting,

entertaining, rigorously dancing with fractured minds
contorted to a joyless pleasure, time sold from life.

The locomotive hums, the prairies hum. Frogs touch
insects with their long tongues, the cannibal fish and
the stabbing birds

wait.

Night actions flash before uncountable animal eyes. Mice
run. Light rain falls in the night.

The frogs are stilled. Between the engine and the sea, the
lights go out. People sleep with mechanical dreams, the sea
hums with rain, the locomotive shines black, fish wait under
the surface of a pinked pool.

Frogs shiver in the cold. The land waits, black, dreaming. Men
lie dry in their beds.

History, history!

Under the closed lids their eyes flick back and forth as they try
to follow the frightening shapes of their desires.

Warm Wind

The wet sun shines a muddy spring,
warm wind blows; I walk, content
with the weather of our hands.

What if the world does end,
and we are only stained shadows
the sidewalk photographed? Today

I hold you and have a happiness
that makes me human once again.

The Flower

I am too tense,
decline to dance
verbally. The flower
is not in its colour,
but in the seed.

George Bowering

The Night Before Morning

With it all over
and you & I
in separate beds
in separated houses,

I think of
Troilus & Cressida
cursing the sun-
rise from their hurricaned bed;

he to clatter away
on his army horse,
she to pick
her sunny way home—

you & I
with nothing touching
but our private thoughts:
mine of poetry,
yours of a strong morning.

Grandfather

Grandfather
         Jabez Harry Bowering
strode across the Canadian prairie
hacking down trees
            and building churches
delivering personal baptist sermons in them
leading Holy holy holy lord god almighty songs in them
red haired man squared off in the pulpit
reading Saul on the road to Damascus at them

Left home
        big walled Bristol town
at age eight
          to make a living
buried his stubby fingers in root snarled earth
for a suit of clothes and seven hundred gruelly meals a year
taking an anabaptist cane across the back every day
for four years till he was whipped out of England

Twelve years old
           and across the ocean alone
to apocalyptic Canada
              Ontario of bone bending child labor
six years on the road to Damascus till his eyes were blinded
with the blast of Christ and he wandered west
to Brandon among wheat kings and heathen Saturday nights
young red haired Bristol boy shoveling coal
in the basement of Brandon college five in the morning

Then built his first wooden church and married
a sick girl who bore two live children and died
leaving several pitiful letters and the Manitoba night

He moved west with another wife and built children and churches
Saskatchewan Alberta British Columbia Holy holy holy
lord god almighty

struck his labored bones with pain
and left him a postmaster prodding grandchildren with crutches
another dead wife and a glass bowl of photographs
and holy books unopened save the bible by the bed

Till he died the day before his eighty fifth birthday
in a Catholic hospital of sheets white as his hair

To Cleave

When I enter you
you enter me.

That is to cleave,

to cling,
cut,

penetrate
& love.

I love you inside
& offer my inside to you.

To cleave is to separate
& join,

to open
& fill.

And I am filled with you
even as I place myself
in our cleft
my love.

The Swing

Renoir's people
        seem to stand
                on a forest floor
of blossoms.

                The girl on the swing
could be fifteen, her dress
        of new flowers.

                        She leans coyly
or thoughtfully away
        from the two men
                with straw hats.

They are artists
        on a Sunday afternoon
                warm in loose clothing,

some kind of wonder
        for the child who
                makes the fourth figure.

She is clasping her empty hands
        in front of her, her head up,
                her eyes the only ones
                looking outward.

Esta Muy Caliente

On the highway
near San Juan del Río
we had to stop the car
for a funeral.

The whole town it was
a hundred people or
two hundred
walking slowly along the highway

toward the yellow domed church
on the top of the hill
and we pulled into the shade
of a shaggy tree.

I turned off the engine
and we heard their music
a screeching saxophone
and high broken noted trumpet

alone and sad in the hot afternoon
as they walked slow like sheep
the women with black shawls
the men in flappy trousers.

Every five minutes the men
threw cherry bombs into the air
behind them: loud gun shots
blasting the afternoon

then the saxophone: tin music
odd tortured jazz
in that mysterious Indian Christian march
up the hill: bearing a coffin to the priest.

It was a small coffin
on the shoulder of one man in front
            the father we thought
the cherry bombs were like violence

against us: but we were stopped.
An old rattling truck

nosed thru them: and they closed
together again behind it
                        ignoring us.

I walked away from the road
in among the bushes and prickly pear
looking for scorpions on the hot sand
and took a leak beside a thin horse.

An hour later the road was clear
and as I got in the car
a man on a donkey came by
a San Juan lonely in the mountains man.

Good afternoon, I said.
Good afternoon, he said, it is very hot.
Yes it is, I said, especially for us.
It is very hot for us too, he said.

News

Every day I add an inch
to the pile of old newspapers
in the closet.

In that three foot pile now
a dozen airliner crashes,
one earthquake in Alaska,
seventeen American soldiers
face down in Asian mud.

I could go on enumerating
like newsprint—we record
violent death & hockey scores
& keep the front room neat.

In front of me, on the table
my empty coffee cup, somewhat melted
butter, carbon copy of an old poem,
familiar things, nothing unexpected.

A plane could crash into the kitchen—
a fissure could jag the floor open—
some olive faced paratrooper bash
his rifle butt thru the window—

It would be news, somewhere.

Circus Maximus

They come
                    each one
of them
            a rise
like those
                who came
before them.

New heroes flexing
to fill the shape
made out for them
by the now dead

but each new man
a refutation of his predecessor.

Camus refining Dostoyevsky
yet feeling the swell
of body the Russian felt

the old man
grizzling in his beard

anticipating the African
who would fit his fingers
over the old pen
playing with down
            on his cheek.

Who knows ten of your molecules
are not in me?

but Nature helps me define
my own shape

looks on as
I stumble over the centuries'
exposed root
lost in my own
                    particularity

(patterns I deny
and that
is part of a pattern).

Styles do not multiply themselves
but are all
pervasive

the suit of clothes
is nothing
without its own disfigurations.

New heroes flex into it
and bend it to their bodies.

Indian Summer

The yellow trees
along the river

are dying I said
they are in
their moment of life
you said.

The Indians I think
are dead, you cant
immortalize them, a
leaf prest between
pages becomes a
page.

In a month
the river will move

beneath ice, moving
as it always does
south. We will
believe it as we

will no longer see
those yellow borders
of the river.

Albertasaurus

The great valley of Drumheller
a silent gorge, filled
with dinosaur bones,

unexpected trees on the plains,
old ghost towns of coal
mines & dinosaurs,

the wood, petrified, the earth
streakt white & brown,
the Badlands, sea shells

caught a thousand miles
from the sea. In the town

small town cafés, restaurants
they say, with Pepsi-Cola neon
signs, old-fashioned menus,

the home of the dinosaur,
caught in a corner of the
prairie, small-town people

in a dying town, conscious
they must cling to the
dinosaur for their living,

cling to his neck, forgetting
where the dinosaur came
to rest.

The House

I

If I describe my house
I may at last describe my self

but I will surely lie
about the house.

For there is the first lie.
It is not a house at all

but a fragment, a share
of a house, instinct drives me

to one door. As certain as
one hair lies beside another.

As certain as these rows of books
carry me from house to house,

arrange me to their will. I
squat for an hour, eye level

to those books, saying I will
read this, or I will read this,

& this way never succeed
in reading my self, no time

left in the hour between
the news & the pants on the floor.

II

In the morning the window
is bamboo & behind that

snow. (But here I am trying
to go outside the house, remember

what I said.) My bare feet
find no wood, the water

runs warm from the tap,
the coffee in the white cup

on which is painted a green
tree. There is a newspaper

on the floor inside the door,
& a woman in the chiffon

of the bed. A salt shaker
of glass & an aluminum

pepper shaker, & in the
farthest room, papers, orderly.

Those are the reason for the house
& its enemy. I am the fisher

who lays his fish side by side
in the pan. The noise of the pen

on paper is the drift of
cigarette smoke in the window's light.

III

The house has a refrigerator
& a stove, a painting & a

husband, & the husband
has fingers from which words

fall as the wine glass falls
unbroken on the rug.

The key fits into the door
as my feet step in snow, cutting

precise patterns & the silence
of wind, & from outside

the windows are glass, &
behind that the house is not empty.

The Egg

The egg sat on the workbench
for weeks, me passing it every day
in my search for tools, cobwebs,
five years old, looking for

the machines of life. The source
of life, I knew, as mysterious as
my mother's bedroom. I didnt touch
the egg for weeks, my brain resembling

its contours. Till the day came
I gave up waiting for the news, I
contrived to make it roll & fall
to the floor beside a rusted shovel.

Bending over, I knew first the
terrible stink, & then the quills
of light, bone, or fiber, it was
a wing never to be used. Its guilt

I carried for a year & then carried
lighter for more years, as if I
myself smelled, as if I had brought
those tender stinking wings to earth.

Dobbin

FOR MIKE ONDAATJE

We found dead animals in our sagebrush hills,
every day it seems now, deer, heads of
unimaginable elk. Or rattlesnake killed
by some kids we likely knew, upside down,
wrong coloured in the burnt couchgrass.

But my first dead horse. It was something
like mother, something gone wrong at home—
his opened & scattered body was tethered,
the old shit surrounded his tufted hair
& his skin, the oil gone, just twisted
leather without eyeballs. A horse, as if
someone had lost him, obeying the rope
thru his open-air starving.

I was then, then, no longer another one
of the animals come to look, this
was no humus like the others, this
was death, not merely dead; that rope
may now hang from some rotted fence.

Our Triple Birth

First by design & later out of
neglect or fear
we have come this far, & myself
furthest without the children
we've already named.

While my sperm dries
year after year, flushes thru drains,
glistens against skin in city after city,
sinks into the earth & coils there
never to stand straight
on its own two feet, a
continuation, my poor rotting skeleton's
rebirth into that heaven
each decade promises
& brings beyond our self-blinded eyes, that
infibulation, that abortion.

That smiling knife-holding gentleman
planted his trees for us, gave us
to name everything we see
& stick it in a book, so even
to name the children coiled only
shrimp in our skull's sea.

& when I'm driven from this garden
I'll leave you there in the earth
to force your own way to sunlight,
Jason, Adam, W. C.

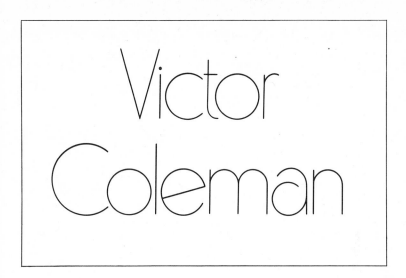

Victor Coleman

The Lady Vanishes

FOR ANN K.

I

The Lady
Vanishes

II

Lovely lady inside your
face my hands move,
in the earth behind
your skin, they dig there
& soil themselves.

          & your eyes?
well, your eyes well up
out of themselves
to make tree colors

                    & your optic
nerve twines tight about
my wrist in there.

III

Oh lady, this moment,
the last one, we are two
children together
dunking our graham crackers in the milk;
& I'm washing it all down
with beer to bring the high down.

My eyes, the gesture of your hands,
change.

IV

The dream saw the mirror
image shatter on the floor
& the image broken up
into its razor syllables.

The dream saw the suicide
then, the wrist or the jugular
cut thru with pieces of
the shattered whole image.

The dream saw the blood there
pucker up from veins,
fall over the wrist to find
its own image.

And the image of the blood
and the image of the lady
vanished, vanishes, was
vanquished in the eye.

v

The lady
The lady vanishes

She does not move
too far out of herself

She does not excite or incite

She vanishes
before my
very very eyes

Kenkyusha: Day Nine

FOR F.W.

*Some poor fellows were trapped by the fire
and were burnt to death, I hear.*

Fred
These messages your father said
Were waiting for us at the cut

& we tripped up there
& caught as you said a ride out
Remember?

Have you asked
'after the fathers of all men?'

I'll ask you now—
How did he like those hockey
games & why didn't you bring him in
to meet us that day you came to pick up
Christmas boots.

                        God I wanted
to meet the man.

The instruction.

The loss of innocence, Fred, the time I was away
& my daughter was born & I called you
on the phone in that confusion

& Pauline told me, or someone, he had
Died. That same day died. I
was that father died.

That same day. The phoneme, Fred, the phone
I called you up on gave instruction of
my daughter's birth, six-thirty a.m.

same time I was sleepily fucking
Abraham's wife in a city neither of us
belongs in.
                        Fred,
I'm asking after your father,
after your father's death
I'm asking you what time

Time, & what were you doing
when he lost his.

The Devil

The horned face
of an ideal

the number fifteen
torch held down

right hand raised in greeting?
A warning

a wariness
warmed to

bat wings against a darkness
that comes from too much light

    Fire in the Man's tail

    Fruit in the Woman's

Perched above & guardian of
their chains

       ram-horned, foul-footed
vision torn from His eyes

Fired or feathered—pointed as two horns
& no direction to give them
proportion

      The Man & the Woman
are naked, their genitals exposed,
chained together at their necks
to the darkness

      The Man speaks
or is doubtful; his gesture
puts the woman in her place

Our innocence naked
or the fire's out of the hearth
into the Man's heart

The Devil holds the fire down

The Man burns warily

The Woman dreams of dancing

Fish : Stone : Song

The salmon swims upstream
into a more perfect pleasure

& the Indian beats it with a stick
shaped like the fish it strikes

& Isaac Paul dreamed a song
which enabled him to catch more cod

& a Nanaimo Salish dreamed he caught
something fierce & the next day caught it

rock in the shape
of that self-same swimmer

which he carried home
laid near where he dreamt it

spoke to him of perseverance
that was prelude to some sound abundance

& told him
rub your hooks upon my surface

whenever the
fisherman becomes inept in you

& he kept it many years   hid in a box
& became that wealthy Indian

like unto a white man
as he grew older

& that stone fish again spoke
in a dream from where he was hid

& told the old fisher
to return to that part of the sea

& find the spot from where he pulled it
& throw it back

                    & the old man did it
finding the place

& having decorated the stone
as the dream voice told him

heaved it in the water
where it behaved in a manner

most unfish-like
more like *lightning*

what gives off to his most great
advantage

Parking Lots for Greg Curnoe

I

Why is Robert Desnos sleeping?

The true radical is any man who will not accept
    the present terms—

No adjustment is needed—if a fly
    is open there is reason—Calamity
    reigns in that area (never been there either)

Too personal, it was always laughing, exchanging
    the unexchangeable glow all over us—

When I do finally come in her mouth there will blossom
    millions tiny tapioca boiling white
    in their own clarity, translucent
    feeling, like joy & jellie babies;
    evident & divers strangers
    swallowed in one or two gulps—

Hot dogs   hot rods   chewing gum wrappers
    all crumpled & torn   blackballs
    Jonnie hand warmers   big little books
    Dick Tracy & Plastic Man   (always cut
    by the villain's broken mirror
    divesting the image   defeated
    by some sharp-edged reflection of
    himself)—

Trading comics with the girl down the street age 9
    huge overbite buck teeth & holey underwear
    kissing me in the closet
    pressing her smelly nineyearold body against mine
    whose teeth push against my tender boy's lips
    still, pulling her pants down for me—

Each one of these doors leads to the present—No engagement
      is needed—the present is yesterday's
      memory sliding in old dead mud
      sad travels & tantamount dreams of reality
      climbing cat's cradle of webs in imagination—
      here today   gone tomorrow—No
      adjustment is needed—

But me   in either case joyous   feeling
      jubilant dew drop from my beard
      on a hill up which we climb
      in the shade of a tree heaved up
      as it is somehow over the road—
      Little lamb who made thee—No adjunct
      is needled—junipers, fat red cedars
      in front of my vision of the world—

Not Kumush   Old man of old men
      trapped inside a wandering adolescence
      sewing from his bag of old dried bones
      collected in serpents' houses   over the land
      so that men might arise from them in tribes—
      the streets & alleyways of his wanderings
      there to perpetrate an image of himself
      A joke   No
      need for readjustment   .   CH'IEN
THE CREATIVE: HEAVEN
                                    in books   old documents
      art & other well-worn dildos
      This man you have invented in your innocence

NO   to your pleas—Need
      Rots—walking   walking
      Oh parochial!

Give me the song of the stout-hearted sucking in
      swoosh of the tea head
      followed by 15 minutes of self contemplation

better than talk about art & the ever
slowly degenerating dollar—a barter
this is my first . . .

Yes   I will buy your violence   but take off that
redress   Move toward an image of heaven
(The Earth)   a vision   Color the atmosphere
ochre if it pleases you

II

'THEN THE PEOPLE BEGAN TO TALK TO THE TREES
AND THE CHANGE CAME'

My fouryearold son spends an hour in the morning arranging
his small pile of books to resemble a silent flat sea—
printer's ink colored & eloquent
upon the adages of its own demise—
that he wanted for his set
of toy vehicles   in the
middle of the living room a parking lot—

Robinson Jeffers entombed in an idea   Dead
anyway   but no more than Ruscha's
portrait of thousands square feet
reduced to the size of each page—
delicate & intricate   Lifeless . . .

I am not complaining I am not complaining   The waning
of the harvest moon is NOT A POEM
(it is a waning

A perfect picture of imbalance in the pause between
this world & the last   .

Realizing that I don't have to talk to people anymore
one syllable words form trains
standing in the station
waiting for people to get on or off—

What you see   paint   is paint   a color
    no sea enters into   No discourse
    of object & fact

Not very interesting artifacts   The mind
    does not live up to any of its promises

III

The gesture of plains in the paintings
    of Georges Braque—locations
    moving in the air   in earth   on air
    projected into the present sense
    ability—the tension
    between us: attention

Something there is that finds two in one   three
    in two   into decisions we made
    about those magic numbers into which
    we have divided ourselves—beyond
    their anti-numerical, over-symbolical
    surfaces towards real qualities
    of the thing, not significant detail—
    the mass of everything—secret
    political prisoners locked in each cell—

The body   of work   is no more ill at ease
    than the work   of the body
    Ask the drugs about their pertinence
    gather your rosebuds where you may
    but sniff too of the air & listen
    to the sounds of worlds colliding
    in the garden   her fingers touching pure joy

Not a scene   (from the movie)   not small
    town   big city   rural route environ
    meant   *the body*   is all we need
    to move through the initial water
    until what holds us breaks

over us & frees us from our chamber—
the trees & intractable mountains
through which no middle-class American
children dance   (too busy sleeping
& playing to dance   'their leisure'
engaged in human relationships—

This   like anything we make
has gone much farther
than I intended—(the man in (?)
Maugham whose pocket's ever full
of enough silver to ensure
the austerity of the spirit)—

The amazing ability of a cabdriver
to articulate over & over each day
the same three phrases from the corner of his mouth
—Moebius stringing the same line—
These lakes were given to us

Drink Me

IV

What are the Rolling Stones talking about
in their music? The future
the torture   the ardure
of living in Britain?   I doubt it.
My belly's not that empty nor my mind.

The amphetamine dreams of resurgence
in blood undermined by Hershey & Nestle—
the beautiful birds of oblivion—

How possibly can a man be a vision
in a world slowly turning
defensively into asbestos & plastic
& bullet-proof alloys of infernal metals.
Licence plates here read: 19BEAUTIFUL68.

The navel's knot   not
center of the earth   however contemplated—
not our intention.

'She comes in colours everywhere'   the real
     'she combs her hair'   explanation
     'she's like a rainbow'   of the music
     of the spheres is not a simile
                                        the plenary abstract
     the word   'colours'   with its optional dipthong
     impotent in the present context:
     darkness.   I have no reason
     to believe in what you're doing
     the unchangeable fact is I do

Since that first show at Moos   was it 1964?
     in the summer heat & cool
     smiling senses of everything's flatness   (from Dorn
     to Zukofsky   without that awareness   a line
     which does not meet any of its points
     at surface) not a thread a wisp   a kiss
     planted on the earth

v

I have taken the liberty of removing your name
     from the long list of great artistic promises
     & readjusting the order in my mind
     to include all those sempiternal gods
     who walk around in our genes like twisted guests—
     the evergreens don't have them
     won't—we inject false light
     into our veins.

I have taken the liberty of advocating the use of drugs
     in the afterlife   (the halflight)   off-white
     spurious & uneventful—addictive
     as anything—heavenly popsicles
     to soothe the heat of dying—

through truth a disease squirms
in our doubts about the world
simply because it *is* so available
A Collage

Surrealism has nothing to do with it—Dada
    is father   a rhythm   I asked
    for a sandwich   they gave me
    delight in a cup—a song
    has nothing to do with it either—
    sing, anyway   Be surreal   Don't
    go mad in the face of their constant
    boredom before so much wonder—
    as long as you've got something
    in your hands besides their currency—
    your empty pockets—you can use them
    please, on others.

Art is a caress   careless & fickle
    as words in our language   lying
    each day for a bit more space—
    an occupation in which we store
    our adored adumbrations.

A compass pointing always in the same direction
    drawn to it   attraction of the
    mercury in my eyes   (the coins)
    slowly replacing our fine bones
    with long brittle members   incapable
    digital fingers & toes   (don't count on them)

A comparison: a line
    of grey paint   /   the horizon

    changing

Gibsons, B.C., 4 September 1968

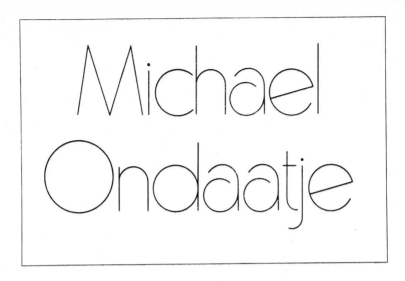

Michael Ondaatje

Early Morning, Kingston to Gananoque

The twenty miles to Gananoque
with tangled dust blue grass
burned, and smelling burned
along the highway
is land too harsh for picnics.
Deep in the fields
behind stiff dirt fern
nature breeds the unnatural.

Escaping cows canter white
then black and white
along the median, forming out of mist.
Crows pick at animal accidents,
with swoops lift meals—
blistered groundhogs, stripped snakes
to arch behind a shield of sun.

Somewhere in those fields
they are shaping new kinds of women.

The Diverse Causes

'for than all erbys and treys renewyth a man and woman,
and in lyke wyse lovers callyth to their mynde olde
jantylnes and olde servyse, and many kynde dedes that
was forgotyn by neclygence'

Three clouds and a tree
reflect themselves on a toaster.
The kitchen window hangs scarred,
shattered by winter hunters.

We are in a cell of civilised magic.
Stravinsky roars at breakfast,
our milk is powdered.

Outside, a May god
moves his paws to alter wind
to scatter shadows of tree and cloud.
The minute birds walk confident
jostling the cold grass.
The world not yet of men.

We clean buckets of their sand
to fetch water in the morning,
reach for winter cobwebs,
sweep up moths who have forgotten to waken.
When the children sleep, angled
behind their bottles, you can hear mice prowl.
I turn a page
careful not to break the rhythms
of your sleeping head on my hip,
watch the moving under your eyelid
that turns like fire,
and we have love and the god outside
until ice starts to limp
in brown hidden waterfalls,
or my daughter burns the lake
by reflecting her red shoes in it.

A House Divided

This midnight breathing
heaves with no sensible rhythm,
is fashioned by no metronome.
Your body, eager
for the extra yard of bed,
reconnoitres and outflanks;
I bend in peculiar angles.

This nightly battle is fought with subtleties:
you get pregnant, I'm sure,
just for extra ground
—immune from kicks now.

Inside you now's another,
thrashing like a fish,
swinging, fighting
for its inch already.

For John, Falling

Men stopped in the heel of sun,
hum of engines evaporated;
the machine displayed itself bellied with mud
and balanced—immense.

No one ran to where
his tensed muscles curled unusually,
where jaws collected blood,
the hole in his chest the size of fists,
hands clutched to eyes like a blindness.

Arched there he made
ridiculous requests for air.
And twelve construction workers

what should they do but surround
or examine the path of falling.

And the press in bright shirts,
a doctor, the foreman scuffing a mound,
men removing helmets,
the machine above him
shielding out the sun
while he drowned
in the beautiful dark orgasm of his mouth.

The Time Around Scars

A girl whom I've not spoken to
or shared coffee with for several years
writes of an old scar.
On her wrist it sleeps, smooth and white,
the size of a leech.
I gave it to her
brandishing a new Italian penknife.
Look, I said turning,
and blood spat onto her shirt.

My wife has scars like spread raindrops
on knees and ankles,
she talks of broken greenhouse panes
and yet, apart from imagining red feet,
(a nymph out of Chagall)
I bring little to that scene.
We remember the time around scars,
they freeze irrelevant emotions
and divide us from present friends.
I remember this girl's face,
the widening rise of surprise.

And would she
moving with lover or husband
conceal or flaunt it,
or keep it at her wrist
a mysterious watch.
And this scar I then remember
is medallion of no emotion.

I would meet you now
and I would wish this scar
to have been given with
all the love
that never occurred between us.

Elizabeth

Catch, my Uncle Jack said
and oh I caught this huge apple
red as Mrs Kelly's bum.
It's red as Mrs Kelly's bum, I said
and Daddy roared
and swung me on his stomach with a heave.
Then I hid the apple in my room
till it shrunk like a face
growing eyes and teeth ribs.

Then Daddy took me to the zoo
he knew the man there
they put a snake around my neck
and it crawled down the front of my dress.
I felt its flicking tongue
dripping onto me like a shower.
Daddy laughed and said Smart Snake
and Mrs Kelly with us scowled.

In the pond where they kept the goldfish
Philip and I broke the ice with spades
and tried to spear the fishes;
we killed one and Philip ate it,
then he kissed me
with raw saltless fish in his mouth.

My sister Mary's got bad teeth
and said I was lucky, then she said
I had big teeth, but Philip said I was pretty.
He had big hands that smelled.

I would speak of Tom, soft laughing,
who danced in the mornings round the sundial
teaching me the steps from France, turning
with the rhythm of the sun on the warped branches,
who'd hold my breast and watch it move like a snail
leaving his quick urgent love in my palm.

And I kept his love in my palm till it blistered.

When they axed his shoulders and neck
the blood moved like a branch into the crowd.
And he staggered with his hanging shoulder
cursing their thrilled cry, wheeling,
waltzing in the French style to his knees
holding his head with the ground,
blood settling on his clothes like a blush;
this way
when they aimed the thud into his back.

And I find cool entertainment now
with white young Essex, and my nimble rhymes.

Peter

I

That spring Peter was discovered, freezing
the maze of bones from a dead cow,
skull and hooves glazed
with a skin of ice.
The warmth in his hands
carved hollows of muscle,
his fingers threading veins on its flank.

In the attempt to capture him
he bit, to defend himself,
three throats and a wrist;
that night villagers found the cow
frozen in red, and Peter
eating a meal beside it.

II

They snared him in evening light,
his body a pendulum
between the walls of the yard,
rearing from shrinking flashes of steel
until they, with a new science,
stretched his heels and limbs,
scarred through the back of his knees
leaving his veins unpinned,
and him singing in the evening air.

Till he fainted, and a brown bitch
nosed his pain, stared in interest,
and he froze into consciousness
to drag his feet to the fountain,
to numb wounds.

III

In the first months of his capture
words were growls, meaningless;
disgust in his tone burned everyone.
At meals, in bed, you heard Peter's howl
in the depths of the castle like a bell.
After the first year they cut out his tongue;

difficult
to unpin a fish's mouth
without the eventual jerk
to empty throat of pin and matter.

There followed months of silence,
then the eventual grunting;
he began to speak with the air of his body,
torturing breath into tones; it was despicable,
they had made a dead animal of his throat.

He was little more than a marred stone,
a baited gargoyle, escaped
from the fountain in the courtyard:
his throat swollen like an arm muscle,
his walk stuttered with limp, his knees straight,
his feet arcing like a compass.

IV

They made a hive for him in the court,
Jason throwing him bones from the table,
the daughter Tara tousling in detail
the hair that collapsed like a nest
over his weaving eyes.
She, with bored innocence,
would pet him like a flower,
place vast kisses on his wrists,
thrilled at scowls and obscenities,
delighted at sudden grins
that opened his face like a dawn.

He ate, bouldered at their feet,
vast hands shaping rice,
and he walked with them on grit drives—
his legs dragged like a suitcase behind him.

v

All this while Peter formed violent beauty.
He carved death on chalices,
made spoons of yawning golden fishes;
forks stemmed from the tongues of reptiles,
candle holders bent like the ribs of men.

He made fragments of people: breasts
in the midst of a girl's stride,
a head burrowed in love,
an arm swimming—fingers heaved
to nose barricades of water.

His squat form, the rippled arms
of seaweeded hair,
the fingers black, bent from moulding silver,
poured all his strength
into the bare reflection of eyes.

VI

Then Tara grew.

When he first saw her, tall,
ungainly as trees,
her fat knees dangled his shoulders
as her hips rode him,
the court monster, she
swaying from side to side, held
only by the grip of her thighs
on his obtuse neck—
she bending over him,
muttering giggles at his eyes,
covering his creased face with her hair.

And he made golden spiders for her
and silver frogs, with opal glares.

And as she grew, her body
burned its awkwardness.
The full bones roamed
in brown warm skin.
The ridge in her back broadened,
her dress hid seas of thighs,
arms trailed to adjust hair that paused
like a long bird at her shoulder;
and vast brown breasts
restless at each gesture
clung to her body like new sea beasts.

And she smiled cool at Peter now,
a quiet hand received gifts from him,
and her fingers, poised,
touched
to generate expressions.

VII

An arm held her, splayed
its fingers like a cross at her neck
till he could feel fear thrashing at her throat,
while his bent hands tore the sheet of skirt,
lifted her, buttock and neck to the table.
Then laying arm above her breasts
he shaped her body like a mould,
the stub of tongue sharp as a cat, cold,
dry as a cat, rasping neck and breasts
till he poured loathing of fifteen years on her,
a vat of lush oil, staining,
the large soft body like a whale.

Then he lay there breathing at her neck
his face wet from her tears
that glued him to her pain.

We're at the Graveyard

Stuart Sally Kim and I
watching still stars
or now and then sliding stars
like hawk spit to the trees.
Up there the clear charts,
the systems' intricate branches
which change with hours and solstices,
the bone geometry of moving from there, to there.

And down here—friends
whose minds and bodies
shift like acrobats to each other.
When we leave, they move
to an altitude of silence.

So our minds shape
and lock the transient,
parallel these bats
who organize the air
with thick blinks of travel:
Sally is like grey snow in the grass.
Sally of the beautiful bones
pregnant below stars.

'The gate in his head'

FOR VICTOR COLEMAN

Victor—the shy mind
revealing faint scars
coloured strata of the brain
not clarity but the sense of shift.
A few lines/the tracks of thought.

The landscape of busted trees
melted tires in the sun
Stan's fishbowl
with a book inside
turning its pages
like some sea animal
camouflaging itself
the typeface clarity
going slow blond in the sun full water

My mind is pouring chaos
in nets onto the page.
A blind lover, dont know
what I love till I write it out.
Then from Gibson's your letter
with a blurred
photograph of a gull.
Caught vision. The stunning white bird
an unclear stir.

And that is all this writing should be then.
The beautiful formed things caught at the wrong moment
so they are shapeless, awkward
moving to the clear.

Postcard from Piccadilly Street

Dogs are the unheralded voyeurs of this world.
When we make love
the spaniel shudders
walks out of the room,
she's had her fill of children now

but the bassett—for whom
we've pretty soon got to find a love object
apart from furniture or visitor's legs—
jumps on the bed and watches.

It is a catching habit having a spectator
and appeals to the actor in both of us,
in spite of irate phone calls from the SPCA
who claim we are corrupting minors
(the dog is one and a half).

We have moved to elaborate audiences now.
At midnight we open the curtains
turn out the light
and imagine the tree outside
full of sparrows
with infra red eyes.

MARGARET ATWOOD

One way of looking at Margaret Atwood's poetry is to see it as the jottings of a pioneer in the uncharted expanses of consciousness. Her poetry seems to say (to make a variation on the Cartesian *cogito ergo sum*), 'I think, therefore I am in trouble.' The human mind is flooded with data that it must edit, arrange, build structures from, in order to retain its sanity, to preserve the distinctions between self and other. As Atwood observes in 'Progressive Insanities of a Pioneer', 'unstructured/space is a deluge'. In this frightening world of cluttered senses, specific objects may assume enormous proportions until they encompass the whole of consciousness. Always there is fear, as expressed in 'A Place: Fragments' (*The Circle Game*), that no key will be found 'that informs, holds together/this confusion, this largeness/and dissolving'.

Another handicap of perception is that it produces isolation or alienation. Men are mere objects in space, separated by manners, modes of perception, differing pasts, their fears, roles, the games they play, the rooms they choose to live in, the objects they collect to give themselves meaning. Atwood's poems reveal an obsession with space—the spaces within, around, and between men and objects. Everywhere there is a barrier between the perceiver and the object perceived, between subject and object; as she says in 'Part of a Day' (*The Animals in That Country*): 'each of us reflects/the despair of the separate/object.' Her poetry is full of skins, cages, glass cases, borders, maps, fortifications, anything that marks the boundaries or demarcations that separate, whether the 'protecting/eggshell' people wear or the nationalities behind which groups hide. Most important, Atwood understands that individuals are alienated from themselves (what is the self but a sequence of illusions?). In 'What Happened' (*Animals*) she speaks of men being locked inside their own catastrophes. As Ken Kesey is reported in *The Electric*

Kool-Aid Acid Test to have said, they are forever doomed to be watching a movie of their own lives. As if the limitations of language were not discouraging enough, we are capable of communicating only 'delayed reactions'. As Atwood suggests in 'Astral Traveller' (*Animals*), not only are men's pasts inaccessible, their very bodies are foreign.

Atwood's technical concerns have far-reaching implications. She is both the archetypal first Canadian, trying to build some shelter or structure against the hostile wilderness, and the archetypal first human walking from the unconscious sleep of evolution. Above all, these perceptual experiments represent modern man's search for identity. Her figures are often pioneers, immigrants, explorers, exiles of one sort or another. Survival is the first necessity for exiles, she says in 'Roominghouse, Winter' (*Animals*). 'We must resist. We must refuse/to disappear.' Like the pioneer, each man must begin by taking an inventory of the trivia, the flotsam of consciousness; he must try to discover meaning where there is no meaning. Poetry is one means of controlling experience, of ordering chaos. Atwood's poems stand as fragments against the flood. She is a careful craftsman. At times she presents her startling, surreal images in a prosaic, matter-of-fact manner that is dislocating to the reader of traditional verse; at other times she assumes absurd points of view, shifts back and forth between reality and fantasy, and uses a variety of other alienating devices including parentheses. She does not hesitate to experiment, to dispense with any device that is predictable and, therefore, potentially boring. Often her line-lengths seem haphazard, questionable, convincing as units of neither sound nor sense; but even here it might be argued that the line-ends serve as unexpected springboards or pulled rugs that draw attention away from music and toward meaning. Most often the poetic mind is so acute and the rapid fire of images so compelling that the prosody itself goes by unnoticed.

Atwood is the author of five books of poetry: *The Circle Game* (1966), which received the Governor General's Award, *The Animals in That Country* (1968), which won first prize in the Centennial Commission competition, *The Journals of Susanna Moodie* (1970), *Procedures for Underground* (1970), containing five poems that received the Union Poetry Prize from *Poetry*, and *Power Politics* (1971). Her novel, *The Edible Woman* (1969), is being made into a film for which she has written the screenplay. She was born in Ottawa in 1939 and has lived in Northern Quebec, Toronto, Boston, Montreal, Vancouver and Edmonton. She is a graduate of the University of Toronto and is completing a PH.D. for Harvard University. She has taught at several universities in Canada and is at present writing full time.

MARGARET AVISON

In 1941 Margaret Avison outlined a modest poetic: 'Literature', she wrote, 'results when: (a) every word is written in the full light of *all* the writer knows; (b) the writer accepts the precise limits of what he knows, i.e.

distinguishes unerringly (while writing) between what he knows, and what he merely knows about, by reputation or reflected opinion.' This poetic, which she endorsed again as recently as 1962, reflects not only the seriousness with which she approaches her craft, but also her view of poetry as a vehicle of discovery. She is a philosophical poet who, like Wallace Stevens, is moved to search for 'truths' that underlie the world we perceive with our senses. She is not a descriptive poet; she is interested, as she explains in 'Voluptuaries and Others', in 'that other kind of lighting up/That shows the terrain comprehended.' 'Nobody stuffs the world in at your eyes,' she says in 'Snow'. 'The optic heart must venture: a jail-break/And re-creation.' In order to make this jail-break, the optic heart must see through the pollution of body and mind that produces a society of unconscious grey men and clapboard suburbs, and 'this communal cramp of understanding' ('The World Still Needs'). In a world where salesmanship is valued more than a fine ear, where limited imaginations triumph, the poet can find little that is worth her attention and respect. The landscapes of *Winter Sun* (1960) are bleak and imprisoning, like the landscapes of Eliot's early poetry; like Eliot also, Avison is often forced to go into the past in search of significant moments of illumination. Thus her interest in great men of science whose imaginative leaps have opened up new worlds of knowledge and experience. 'History makes the spontaneous jubilation at such moments less and less likely though,' she laments.

Avison's epistemological concerns have resulted in a number of poems that explore the nature of imaginative perception. Many poems in *Winter Sun* are characterized by rapid shifts of perspective, a kind of poetic equivalent of the use of multiple lenses and camera-angles in film-making. To write in the 'full light of *all* the writer knows' involves dispensing with all formal notions of time and space. As in the stream-of-consciousness novel, the reader of Avison's poetry is often hard-pressed to find a centre of gravity, a fixed point of reference. It is as though, in this world of continuous change, the only certainty is the act of perception itself. Each new poem, for poet and reader alike, is analogous to the swimmer's moment at the whirlpool; if both 'dare knowledge', they will discover perhaps 'the silver reaches of the estuary'.

The austere winter terrain of her first book gives way to gentler landscapes and warmer climates in *The Dumbfounding* (1966), marking a deepening of religious experience. There is also a reconciliation with the physical world that results in poetry at once more concrete and sensuous. These poems are characterized by a careful observation of minutiae, such as the faces of loiterers and the industry of ants; it is the work of a poet fully absorbed in actuality. Here Avison leaves behind most of the rhetorical and esoteric elements that trouble her earlier verse; her sensitivity to the subtleties of language now encompasses the sound of raindrops, 'letting the ear experience this/discrete, delicate/clicking.'

Margaret Avison was born in Galt, Ont., in 1918 and educated at the University of Toronto. She has been a librarian, a secretary, a research worker, a lecturer in English literature, and is presently engaged in social work at a mission in downtown Toronto. She is one of the finest but least prolific poets in Canada. Apart from the two books mentioned, her poems have appeared mainly in magazines and anthologies. During the early forties and fifties she contributed to Sid Corman's *Origin*, along with Charles Olson, Denise Levertov, and Robert Creeley. Other than giving occasional readings and participating in a writers' workshop at the University of British Columbia, she has remained at the edges of the literary arena in Canada. She is an enthusiastic supporter of other writers and has translated a number of poems from the Hungarian.

EARLE BIRNEY

Birney is a man of great humanity and conscience who has always believed that moral progress is possible. As he says in 'Conference of Heads', 'There is no fog but in the will/the iceberg is elective.' However, his observation of the scarred battleground of his own century has troubled him deeply, causing him to lash out in anger at human cruelty and indifference and to despair at his own guilt and complicity. These two responses reflect the Marxism of a generation caught in two world wars and a depression as well as the Puritanism of his heritage. The first accounts for his well-known vitriolic satires, such as 'Anglo-Saxon Street', and for his more recent attacks on the economic and political atrocities of the American empire, such as 'Sinaloa' and 'Images in Place of Logging', where he describes 'the men and the metalled/ ants that multiply in the browning/pulp of the peeled world.' More convincing than the poems of moral outrage are his poems of guilt and initiation, such as 'David', 'For George Lamming', and 'Arrivals'. In 'Arrivals' he participates in the gratuitous death of a young lawyer whose car has collided with a passenger train. Seeing the outstretched hand, the poet wonders, 'is it only in me that the hand hooked/and I who must manage it now like a third?' As early as 1945, Birney had written from Watford Military Hospital lamenting the time-bomb within each man, and pleading: 'O men be swift to be mankind/or let the grizzly take.' Almost twenty years later, he wrote in 'Letter to a Cuzco Priest': 'Pray to yourself above all for men like me/that we do not quench/the man in each of us.'

In 'The Bear on the Delhi Road', Birney suggests the method by which he brings his world under imaginative control. He says: 'It is not easy to free/ myth from reality.' He describes the business of trying to make a bear dance —that is, giving it human form by making it dance rather than merely amble among berries. The men of Kashmir are like the poet, trying to transform crude reality, trying to give it artistic shape. The process seems to be a characteristic one for Birney. He begins with the real and concrete, whether an object or an experience, and reflects upon it until its 'meaning' (for him) is released. This is the essential structure of the romantic ode, wherein the poet contemplates a height of land (say Tintern Abbey) and is moved to discover some personal and universal significance in his experience. It is certainly the organizing principle at work in 'Vancouver Lights', 'A Walk in Kyoto', and many of Birney's travel poems; and it is a method he shares quite noticeably with Al Purdy.

Birney's energies have always been engaged in coming to terms with his need for a social identity and with his separateness as an artist. Despite his involvement in the war and the universities, he has always been an outsider, beset by internal and external forces that have kept him from feeling fulfilled. He resents society's indifference to the artist and feels intensely that the artist has a cure for society's ills. In 'Cartagena de Indias' he describes what it means to learn that other cultures can honour even their most critical poets. 'I love the whole starved cheating/poetry-reading lot of you,' he says of the Colombians, 'I who am seldom read by my townsmen.' In *The Creative Writer*, Birney speaks of the situation of the writer in Canada:

> It seems to me that the effective writer is one who is inwardly sure of the entire naturalness of his creative act. For instance, he must be aware that he is writing not merely because he is neurotic. Everybody's a bit queer and slightly mad, but I'm sure that my compulsion to construct more and more unprofitable verses isn't anywhere near as screwball as the compulsion of businessmen to make more and more money. But the writer who does not believe this is hamstrung from the start, haunted by a false diagnosis of his society, and driven either into a permanent state of apology and mock-modesty for his abnormality, or into snarling hatred for the nastiness of the normal.

This describes accurately many of the tensions Birney has felt during his own lifetime. One of his ways of counteracting this feeling of apartness has been to try to transform the university into a place where creativity can flourish. After years of battling, Birney finally succeeded in bringing into existence the Department of Creative Writing at the University of British Columbia. For Birney there can be no real resolution of this tension. And there is reason to believe that without it his peculiar *daimon* would cease to function. That is why he is continually on the move, why he is always experimenting in his art.

'Living art,' Birney says, 'like anything else, stays alive only by changing.' His own verse has travelled from the most traditional beginnings—including narrative, meditative lyrics, satires, nature poems, and odes—through years of experiment with typography and orthography, down the long congested road to concrete poetry. Birney is a constant reviser of poems and a contributor to little magazines. 'I don't know exactly where the literary Dew Line is this moment,' he says, 'but I'm sure it lies somewhere in the complicated world of today's little-little magazines and small-press chapbooks.'

Birney's life is as colourful as his art—and as controversial. He was born in 1904 in Calgary, but spent most of his youth in Banff and in Creston, B.C.

He graduated from the University of British Columbia in 1926. His graduate studies in California were interrupted by difficulties, mostly financial, which took him to Utah to teach, and to New York to work for the Trotskyites. With a grant from the Royal Society he completed his doctoral studies in London, Eng., and at the University of Toronto, where he lectured for several years and served as literary editor of the *Canadian Forum*. During the Second World War he was a Personnel Selection Officer overseas and then for a short time was Supervisor of Foreign Language Broadcasts to Europe for the CBC. Later he joined the English Department at UBC and was head of the Department of Creative Writing. Recently he has been poet-in-residence at universities in Canada and the United States and has travelled widely.

Birney's reputation as a poet was established with *David and Other Poems* (1942) and *Now Is Time* (1945), for both of which he won a Governor General's Award. Further books have followed, including *The Strait of Anian: Selected Poems* (1948), *Trial of a City and Other Verse* (1952), *Ice Cod Bell or Stone* (1962), *Near False Creek Mouth* (1964), *Selected Poems* (1966), and *Rag and Bone Shop* (1970). Birney has also written two novels, *Turvey* (1949), which won the Stephen Leacock medal for humour, and *Down the Long Table* (1955), and a series of lectures prepared for the CBC, *The Creative Writer* (1966).

GEORGE BOWERING

A good deal of nonsense, most of it propaganda masquerading as aesthetics, has been written and spoken about Bowering's poetry, especially his association with Charles Olson and other poets of Black Mountain College. It is true that Bowering has learned from Olson to reject the closed form in poetry, with its clichés of thought and manner, in favour of the open form, or what Olson calls 'composition by field'. Olson insists that a poem is a *thing*, a unit of energy passed from writer to reader, and that it has its own laws, the most important being that form and content must unfold simultaneously, grow out of each other. The other side of 'objectism' is that the poet himself is a thing, an object, and must continually face the fact of his existence in the physical world. He must begin with the literal fact of being; thus his preoccupation with his breathing, the rhythms of his body, the objects he has contact with. It is not so much Bowering's subscription to this poetic, however, as his identification with certain anarchic elements in the American tradition that troubles his readers.

Bowering's primitivism involves certain Dionysian gestures that one associates with Irving Layton: the urge to throw off the yoke of tradition, the use of barbarisms, the rejection of familiar poetic devices such as rhyme, metrics, alliteration, and the simile. What is usually ignored by critics is that this poetic, or anti-poetic, which is just one of many stances towards reality, has its roots not in America but in English romanticism. Wordsworth, not Whitman, provided the first major thrust towards the democratization of art.

Bowering is aware that his poetic is no more than a single pattern imposed on experience to make it tolerable. In 'Circus Maximus' he speaks of being 'lost in my own particularity', but subsequently admits: '(pattern I deny/and that/is part of a pattern)'. It is not surprising that Bowering, whose energies were once channelled into the publication of a magazine with the outrageously anagrammatical title of *Tish*, should be drawn to an aesthetic that serves as a healthy antidote for his academic existence and for the conforming, repressing elements at work in his society.

Many of Bowering's comments about technique relate to the question of *voice*. 'Not just Wordsworth's vague idea of using common speech,' he says, 'but *how to get your own voice on the page*.' In his recent book on the poetry of Al Purdy, Bowering explains the notion of finding your own voice as 'a writing-school aphorism that inadequately describes the process whereby the poet comes to avail himself of ways to get the individualities of his speech habits into his prosody.' Or, in Creeley's (and Olson's) words: 'Speech is an assertion of one man, by one man, "Therefore each speech having its own character, the poetry it engenders will be peculiar to that speech also in its own intrinsic form."'

There is no one way to achieve this end. Bowering rejects all the familiar trappings in favour of a 'plain style' consisting of vocabulary and sentence structure that are casual and simple. He avoids the phrasally determined line and the line that is always a unit of sound and sense. His irregularly determined lines and use of syncopation free his verse from the tedium of easily anticipated line breaks, but occasionally the conversational style he aims for results in a certain flatness. The relation between 'voice' and prosody may be closer to Wordsworth than Bowering admits; after all, the question still rests in the poet's choice between his tired breakfast voice and his animated evening voice. Yeats settled the matter for himself by claiming to be interested only in passionate normal speech.

The poet's work is also affected by his notion of subject. If he begins always with the fact of his own being, he may perhaps get no further. Alden Nowlan states the dangers in this way:

> The most vulnerable part of poetry born of immediate experience is its tendency to slide into banality, where the incident or subject itself does not seem to the reader to have warranted the importance attached to it by the poet.

Many of Bowering's poems, especially those about sex or intimate feelings, get bogged down in the perceiving consciousness, so that what seems to have been the impetus for the poem is lost. One way of explaining this is to say not that the subjective aesthetic is at fault but that the subject itself has not been sufficiently 'worked up'. Bowering's best poems go beyond ego; they break away to take on an existence, a reality, of their own. In these poems he engages in considerable naming, or cataloguing, of things, events, and people in his immediate environment. In 'A Comment on the Singular', he says: 'To name is to begin to admit.' To admit what? To admit that there is poetry hidden away in words, in their sounds and meanings, if the poet can find the context that will release it. Perhaps to admit, finally, that poetry is about words themselves. That is why he considers the simile a means of 'treating' a subject rather than of 'finding out the melodies and significances that objects can reveal once the imagination finds its place among them.'

Bowering was born in Penticton, B.C. in 1935. He completed a B.A. in History and an M.A. in English at the University of British Columbia. As well as being an editor of *Tish*, a controversial little magazine on the west coast, he did the usual odd jobs that poets do to support themselves between sessions at the desk, at college, and at the pub. He was in the RCAF for a while and travelled to Mexico, where, he says: 'I first saw strangers as individuals. I got close to people and that has always been a hard thing for me: to be close to people.' He taught at the University of Alberta before moving to Montreal, where he teaches at Sir George Williams University and edits his own magazine, *Imago*.

Bowering's publications include *Sticks & Stones* (1963), *Points on the Grid* (1964), *The Man in Yellow Boots* (1965), *The Silver Wire* (1966), *Baseball* (1967), *Two Police Poems* (1968), and his two Governor-General's-Award-winning books, *Rocky Mountain Foot* (1969) and *The Gangs of Kosmos* (1969). He has also published a novel, *Mirror on the Floor* (1967), and a book of literary criticism, *Al Purdy* (1970).

LEONARD COHEN

The movement of Cohen's poetry is toward greater simplicity, toward verse that is free of artifice and the colouring of the individual ego. Speaking of these changes, Cohen says: 'Well, you know, you get wiped out. And the deeper the wipe-out, the deeper the reluctance to use ornament or to use any other faculties that brought you to the wipe-out.' In 'Style', a poem that is central to his work aesthetically and pyschologically, Cohen hints at the potential for brotherhood and harmony existing (in an electric reality that could be either Buddha's or Marshall McLuhan's) beyond the trappings of ego, culture, and nationalism. The search for a 'plain' style in poetry does not mean simply the slap-it-all-down manner that characterizes so much recent writing. It suggests rather a desire to eliminate all clichés of thought and expression that could interfere with the poet's efforts to give imaginative expression to his vision of things. In Cohen's own words:

> I think that a decent man who has discovered valuable secrets is under some obligation to share them. But I think that the technique of sharing them is a great study....
>
> Now, you can reveal secrets in many ways. One way is to say this is the secret I have discovered. I think that this way is often less successful because when that certain kind of conscious creative mind brings itself to bear on this information, it distorts it, it makes it very inaccessible. Sometimes it's

just in the voice, sometimes just in the style, in the length of the paragraph; it's in the tone, rather than in the message.

Cohen has learned many ways to share his secrets. In *Let Us Compare Mythologies*, the first book in the McGill Poetry Series, and *Spice-Box of Earth* he wrote in a traditional manner but was able to surprise his readers with unexpectedly bizarre images and witty about-faces. He experiments with the surreal, the lyrical, and the anti-poetic. Here Cohen explores in a light, youthful manner the mysteries and paradoxes of the Jewish and Christian religions. He also reveals a romantic obsession with regeneration and transcendence through varieties of physical love, sacrifice, violence, and degradation that ultimately finds its fullest statement in *Beautiful Losers*. The tone of joyous celebration gives way in *Flowers for Hitler* to darker imaginings. This book is Cohen's dark night of the soul. He discovers his heart of darkness in the Nazi atrocities of the Second World War; he descends morally and imaginatively into the fiery furnaces of Belsen and Auschwitz where, like Conrad's Marlow, he comes face to face with his own emptiness, his own capacity for evil.

At times, when Cohen is too close to his subject, when the materials seem to call for irony or some other distancing technique, Cohen tries unsuccessfully to speak in his own voice. However, he is at his best when he adopts the obliqueness of symbolism rather than direct statement (of the kind found in Bowering's verse, for example). As F. says in *Beautiful Losers*, 'We who cannot dwell in the Clear Light must dwell in Symbols.' Cohen has a unique capacity for creating weird psychological parables, such as 'Story', 'You Have the Lovers', and a number of the recorded songs. Among popular contemporary lyrics, Cohen's songs most closely resemble the symbolic narratives of Bob Dylan. The symbolic mode suits Cohen well; it is like the Buddhist notion of the beautiful answer that asks a more beautiful question.

Cohen's life style is consistent with the directions of his art. He was born in 1934 into a wealthy, cultured family, complete with chauffeur and governess, in Montreal's Westmount district. After barely passing the supplemental examinations he graduated from McGill and went on to an abortive three-week venture in graduate studies at Columbia University. Cohen returned to Montreal to read in night clubs, to write *Ballet of Lepers* (a novel that was never published), and to try a stint in the family clothing business. Eventually he received a Canada Council grant to go to England, where he worked on his first published novel, *The Favourite Game*. From England he set out for Greece and the island of Hydra, where he wrote much of his poetry and fiction and where he lived in creative seclusion with Marianne. Cohen has since returned to Montreal and New York to take up a full-time career as a composer-singer. He has had two albums of songs produced by Columbia Records: *Leonard Cohen* and *Songs from a Room*. Despite his considerable success as a performer, he lives a quiet, almost ascetic life. When his *Selected Poems* was awarded the Governor General's Award, Cohen wrote to say:

May I respectfully request that my name be withdrawn from the list of recipients of the Governor-General's Award. . . . I do sincerely thank all those concerned for their generous intention. Much in me strives for this honor but the poems themselves forbid it absolutely.

Cohen has recently made a concert tour of England and Europe that may mark the beginning of a more public career.

His publications include *Let Us Compare Mythologies* (1956), *Spice-Box of Earth* (1961), *Flowers For Hitler* (1964), *Parasites of Heaven* (1966), and *Selected Poems, 1956-1968* (1968). His two novels are *The Favourite Game* (1963) and *Beautiful Losers* (1966).

VICTOR COLEMAN

Victor Coleman was born in 1944 in Toronto and grew up there and in Montreal. He dropped out of secondary school, married at age eighteen, and worked at odd jobs to support his family and his writing. He submitted to a variety of little magazines and edited *Island* (which ran to eight issues). For short periods he was a production assistant at the Oxford University Press and a linotype operator for *The Coast News* in Gibsons, B.C. At present he is living at Rochdale College in Toronto with his second wife, Sarah, editing *Is*, and working as editor and production manager of The Coach House Press. He attended the Berkeley Poetry Conference with Jack Spicer, Charles Olson, Gary Snyder, Robert Duncan, Allen Ginsberg, Robert Creeley, and others, and is one of the poets reading in The New American Poetry Circuit for 1970-1. His publications include *From Erik Satie's Notes to the Music* (1965), *one/eye/love* (1967), *Light Verse* (1969), and *America* (1971).

Coleman has always insisted on going his own way. He does not subscribe to the poetics of Black Mountain College, or to the 'realist' and 'myth-making' fashions in Canada. Coleman's tastes as an editor are catholic: the early issues of *Island* contain poems by Newlove, MacEwen, Bowering, Souster, and Purdy. He reads and is willing to learn from such contemporaries as Jack Spicer and Charles Olson, but remains very much his own poet. His earliest poetry is often personal and idiosyncratic to the point of being inaccessible, but it is seldom without interest. The one characteristic that persists throughout his still short career as a poet is a disarming playfulness. He has always had a more than mild obsession with rhymes, internal and external, and with alliteration, as is evident in this early poem, 'a song', from *Island #3*:

> *sung as the shrill*
> *bird . the word*
> *offers the ear*
> *cheer, as it be*
> *to be the chor-*
> *us for us, &*
> *by our sense of*
> *hear, as ear, here*

This kind of playfulness, this delight in language, is a great asset to a young poet, because it enables him to learn about the essentials of the craft instead of striving unduly for meaning or statement that is beyond his experience.

Robert Duncan expressed considerable delight in Coleman's *Light Verse*, and in the fact that the book is dedicated to Jack Spicer: 'Always such an intense, intent, thereness to the line that all the emotion is true to the poem. It's that, something more than authenticity, that Jack insisted upon. . . . it is a rare poet who comes thru for me bringing such a delite, winning me to whole-hearted reading.' The *thereness* Duncan speaks of refers not only to the consistent intelligence that informs the poetry, but also to the linguistic and typographical precision with which the poems are made. Coleman concerns himself not merely with the fantastic image or the profound thought (though these may come naturally to a poem), but rather with a maximum use of every word. In Coleman's poems there are no second-class words; if placed in the right context, or position, the most common word may be made to give out new energies or meanings. Articles, prepositions, suffixes may jump off the page by virtue of being given prominence in a line. It is a poetry directed more to the ear than to the eye or to the mind, so there is no need in a single poem for verbs and nouns and adjectives to crowd out other parts of speech. In this way Coleman not only increases the linguistic resources at his disposal, but also pulls the reader more intimately into the actual texture of sounds in the poem, rather than sending him off on analytical cul-de-sacs.

Although he does not eschew the most useful of the age-old poetic techniques, Coleman has been reluctant to accept the closed form. Readers are fascinated by his break-away from the notion of the poem as a set-piece, and the notion of a feeling or experience as a 'subject' to be worked up. In *one/eye/love* and *Light Verse* he is somehow able to hold together within a single imaginative context an unusually wide range of diction and feeling. The poem does not have to have a consistent mood, or stick to a single theme. This open-endedness, or inclusiveness, is often mistaken for incompetence, but to careful readers it should prove a relief from the far too familiar cross-fertilization of metaphor and miniature Aristotelian anecdotes that work up to a punch-line or bogus catharsis.

Allen Ginsberg speaks of Coleman's poems as 'improvizations'. In a letter to Coleman he says: 'Read *Parking Lots*—was thumbing thru *radiofreerainforest* I saw the line "I have taken the liberty . . . afterlife" which was so odd and intelligent I went back to the beginning. The whole poem or spout was funny & of lovely nature. There aren't many improvizations I can read with detail & humour any more & this poesy was *interesting*. . . .' Improvization is a good term, especially for its associations with jazz. Coleman's ear and imagination explore a word or a phrase in much the same way that a jazz musician searches out the contours of a note or musical phrase—pushing the phrase in a number of directions, building on it, using it as a springboard. In one of his recent poems, 'America', Coleman has invented his own equivalent of the closed form. In each section he accepts the limitations of a tarot card randomly drawn (e.g., the NINE OF SWORDS), the first word in each line beginning with the corresponding letter from the card. This formal limitation frees him, as the sonnet freed the Elizabethan poet, to discover new combinations of sound and sense.

'We make up a different language for poetry/And for the heart—ungrammatical', Coleman says in 'Transformations II'. In his search for a new language he does not sit still; his discoveries influence him, make him rethink his poetic directions. But he is self-taught, so his discoveries and subsequent developments come with surprise and delight and, of course, a certain roughness, which is a small price to pay for poetry that escapes the tiring slickness of a professional imitation.

D. G. JONES

Doug Jones was born in Bancroft, Ont., in 1929 and educated at McGill and Queen's Universities. He began writing as an undergraduate at McGill, where he won a number of prizes in creative writing. His early work was encouraged and ultimately published by Louis Dudek and Raymond Souster in magazines and in book form by Contact Press. Jones has taught at several universities in Canada and is a member of the English department at the University of Sherbrooke, where he is an editor of *Ellipse*, a quarterly review designed to present the work of French and English writers in translation. He has published three books of poetry—*Frost on the Sun* (1957), *The Sun is Axeman* (1961), and *Phrases from Orpheus* (1967)—and a major analysis of image and theme in Canadian literature, *Butterfly on Rock* (1970). He lives with his wife and children in North Hatley, Que.

There is a passage in *Butterfly on Rock* that is both an acute comment on the state of poetry in Canada and a useful summary of Jones's own poetic development: 'Having reached the Pacific, Canadians have begun to turn back on themselves, to create that added dimension Teilhard de Chardin calls the noosphere.... more than ever before, we have arrived at a point where we recognize, not only that the land is ours, but that we are the land's.' Jones's three volumes of poetry represent the stages in his own journey towards a 'true' landscape. In *Frost on the Sun* Jones was preoccupied with violence and disintegration, but only as poetic *subjects*, not as pressing realities that must find poetic resolution. In *The Sun is Axeman*, however, a hostile nature is presented, one that is stunted and barren, mute and unsympathetic, unlike anything in the pastoral world of his early poems. Many of the poems present the unpredictable landscapes of dreams, landscapes that may splinter into betrayal and degeneration. 'Little Night Journey' is a Whitmanesque symbolic narrative that suggests rather than describes the violence lurking beneath the still surface of consciousness. In *Phrases From Orpheus* Jones experiences some sort of dark night of the soul, arrives at his own underworld. This is Jone's *Flowers for Hitler*, his descent into the heart of darkness, in which he asks: 'how shall I love/this earth,/which is my certain death?' 'All earth is now an underground', he says in 'En Guise d'Orphée'. Jones feels in all things a potential for violence, for disintegration, but he understands this at a psychological level to be a fundamental aspect of reality. In the later poems, myth functions not as ornament but as a controlling structural element; these poems are successful, not because they rewrite old myths, but because they reveal something of the poet's own world. In a letter to the editors, Jones wrote: 'It is always a case of seeing through a conventional pattern or faded myth to something more immediate, vital or violent, and the renewal of the old or the creation of a new myth more adequate to that immediate experience.' *Orpheus* also includes a number of poems that grow out of very personal emotional experience, but experience that is controlled and manipulated. These poems are extremely well turned and yet they retain a psychological depth that is quite remarkable.

As important as Jones's discovery of his own noosphere is his discovery of the means with which to give it imaginative expression. In 'Clotheslines' he argues that

> *the most common things*
> *clothes hung out to dry*
> *serve as well as kings*
> *for your imagery.*

The truth is that common things serve *better* than kings, as Jones discovers in *The Sun is Axeman*. His early poetry had been too general, too abstract. The sense of logic, or intellect, was oppressive; too often sound and image were under severe strain from having to flesh-out the skeleton of thought that held a poem together. However, in poems such as 'Portrait of Anne Hébert' and 'For Françoise Adnet', the images grow with the poem; they are not grafted on. The metaphors are organic, drawing the reader toward, rather than away from, the subject. Jones begins to use common objects quite naturally and his poetry makes its appeal through the senses, not merely through the intellect. He forsakes his idealized landscapes for the colour and texture of the actual world around him.

Jones's concern for a more personal, affective style is not limited to imagery. In 'A Problem of Space' he suggests the directions he would like his poetry to take. 'I would eliminate this bombast, this/Detail of type,' he says, 'and leave an image/And a space'. The search for a more precise and more immediate form of expression took him briefly to Pound and the Imagists and then to moderns such as Auden. In 'Portrait of Anne Hébert' the language is natural, the syntax simple and insistent, suggesting that the poet is too caught up in the *making* to be fanciful or verbose. Here, and in the more complicated poems of *Phrases from Orpheus*, Jones is concerned with 'articulating a highly intense and obscure complex of feelings with extreme economy . . . with a certain simplicity and yet dramatic power.' One poem that seems to realize this difficult goal is 'These Trees Are No Forest of Mourners'; it has a sureness and a simplicity that are quite striking. The best of Jones's later poems have this sculptural quality, this sharpness of outline. Their success lies not in an exhaustiveness of detail, but rather in their precision and economy of phrasing. We are left, as in the Chinese paintings that Jones admires, with only an image—and a space in which that image can grow.

IRVING LAYTON

Layton is the best-known and most controversial figure in Canadian poetry, because he is so outspoken and graphic in his denunciations. Like Auden, he believes that the writing of poetry is a political act; as he explains in the Preface to *The Laughing Rooster*:

> In this country the poet has always had to fight for his survival. He lives in a middle-class milieu whose values of money-getting, respectability, and success are hostile to the kind of integrity and authenticity that is at the core of his endeavour. His need to probe himself makes him an easy victim for those who have more practical things to do—to hold down a job, amass a fortune, or to get married and raise children. His concern is to change the world; at any rate, to bear witness that another besides the heartless, stupid, and soul-destroying one men have created is possible.

Layton's barbs are not limited to the middle-class. He is equally critical of educational institutions. He rejects Culture as 'that underarm perspiration odour of impotent old men'; and he describes good taste as 'something to wipe our unstodgy behinds with'.

Layton is a man of contradictions. He would have us believe that he is a 'brawling, irreverent', wild-eyed poet with no use for conservative values. Despite his swagger and cultivated disdain, however, Layton is neither a primitive nor a sensualist. His satire, bombast, and erotica are the masks for his fine, beleaguered sensibility. His need to project an image of controversy has often made him espouse issues and causes that seem inconsistent with his expressed poetic vision, with the vision of poetry as freedom. Perhaps it is a comment on our country, rather than on Layton, that his second-rate poems of social gesture should attract more attention than his most delicate, refined verse. A society that destroys its water, forests, and air is not likely to conserve its precious resources of imagination; it will only drive joy and lyricism underground and build expressways over them.

If Layton himself remains an enigma, his literary significance is more certain. Like Whitman in the United States, he has done much to stimulate interest in poetry and to loosen its choking collar. He has reminded us that there are no inherently unpoetic subjects—there are only unpoetic minds. Poetry, he says, is 'a self-authenticated speaking, a reaching down into the roots of one's being'. The poet is someone who knows 'the terror and ecstasy of living daily beyond one's psychic means'. Layton is a conscious craftsman, but he insists that 'without the material given the poet when his Unconscious (soul) is stirred into activity by a powerful emotion, his intelligence and craftsmanship are of no use to him whatever'. His own best poems are a perfect blend of passion and restraint, of a conscious and an unconscious ordering of materials.

Layton's poetry is concerned with three main subjects: sexual love, power, and imagination. Like most men he is attracted to the subject of large-scale expenditures of energy, especially violence. He believes that men are basically aggressive and that battles and wars are a means of psychic cleansing. Sexual love is, for Layton, another form of encounter that has its creative and destructive aspects. His poetic treatment of sex would hardly meet with the approval of the Women's Liberation Movement. Man can dominate reality, Layton tells us in 'The Fertile Muck', not only by love, but also by imagination. Art is the supreme synthesizer; it can contain paradox and contradiction because it deals with the truth that lies between opposites, as we have learned from poets like Blake and Yeats. As Layton explains in 'The Birth of Tragedy': 'Love, power, the huzza of battle/are something, are much;/yet a poem includes them like a pool/water and reflection.'

Layton was born in Romania in 1912. While a child he went with his parents to Montreal, where he has spent most of his life. He studied agricultural science at Macdonald College and economics at McGill University. He taught in a boys' private school before taking up his teaching position at Sir George Williams University. In the forties Layton was associated with Louis Dudek and John Sutherland in the editing of *First Statement*, a controversial magazine that later merged with *Preview* to become *Northern Review*. In the fifties he joined with Dudek and Raymond Souster in the founding of the influential Contact Press. Since then Layton has taught, travelled, edited books, read his poetry on campuses across the country, and been an active commentator on current affairs. He is now a professor of English at York University.

Since the publication of *Here and Now* (1945), Layton has published many books of poetry, including *The Improved Binoculars* (1956), *A Red Carpet for the Sun* (1959), for which he received the Governor General's Award, *Balls for a One-Armed Juggler* (1963), *The Laughing Rooster* (1964), *Collected Poems* (1965), *Periods of the Moon* (1967), *The Shattered Plinths* (1968), and *The Whole Bloody Bird* (1969). Some of his short stories are included in *The Swinging Flesh* (1961). He has also edited *Love Where the Nights Are Long: Canadian Love Poems* (1962).

GWENDOLYN MacEWEN

Many modern poets reveal their self-consciousness about the process of writing by making this a subject for their poetry. Artistic self-consciousness may be the product of living in a culture that questions the value of art; it may also be a product of the general self-consciousness of the times that makes people, artists and others alike, question every activity and motive of

their lives. Aestheticians might say that a preoccupation with process reflects only the necessary understanding that in art there is nothing to be said,
only ways of saying it. Gwendolyn MacEwen is not of this persuasion. For a
young poet, she writes with surprising confidence in her own capacities and
in the authenticity of her undertaking. She rejects self-indulgent, therapeutic
poetry and the 'terribly cynical and "cool" poetry written today'. She believes that the poet can and must say things; and she writes with the conviction that she has discovered things sayable, and worth saying. 'I write
basically to communicate joy, mystery, passion,' she says,' . . . not the joy
that naively exists without knowledge of pain, but that joy which arises out
of and conquers pain. I want to construct a myth.'

MacEwen's poetry might well be discussed in terms of the peculiar ground
it inhabits between the 'realists' and the 'myth-makers' in Canadian poetry.
From the beginning she has repudiated the actual world for one that is
ancient and mythic, believing that imagination can reconcile the antinomies
in life. 'I believe there is more room inside than outside,' she says in the
introduction to *A Breakfast for Barbarians*. 'And all the diversities which
get absorbed can later work their way out into fantastic things, like hawk-
training, IBM programming, mountain-climbing, or poetry.' Like Blake and
Yeats, she draws her inspiration from things occult, mystical, rather than
from traditional mythology. She is most alive to the myth and ritual contained in ordinary experience; her motorcycle Icarus bears little resemblance
to the original. Her landscapes and figures are mostly dream-like, not bound
by normal conventions of space and time; her characters are symbolic, their
movements ritualistic.

'I am involved with writing as a total profession, not as an aesthetic
pursuit,' she says. 'My prime concern has always been with the raw materials from which literature is derived, not with literature as an end in
itself.' Of course one of the primary sources of raw material for the writer
is literature itself. MacEwen has long been preoccupied with the figure
of the artist, whether the Egyptian scribes 'who drew/eyes right into their
hieroglyphs' or the solitary figure of the dancer. As she says in 'Finally Left
in the Landscape',

> Yet still I journey to this naked country
> to seek a form which dances in the sand.
> This is my chosen landscape.

She chooses this landscape but not without certain misgivings, as she
suggests in 'Poems in Braille'. Here she expresses the conflict she feels
between art and life, between the world of names and the world of things,
between dance and action. For her, as for the Platonist, things are but the
shadows of a real world. Words, the names we give to things, are more real
because they are our attempt to describe the other-worldliness of things;
they are the windows through which we view reality. However attractive
this landscape, the poet cannot help but doubt its sufficiency at times. Mac-
Ewen is aware that the whole of the message may not be contained in the

medium, that it may be found in the very *things* she eschews. 'I do not read the long cabbala of my bones/truthfully', she admits. She asks to follow Wenceslas, who could behold a peasant gathering fuel and be moved and involved in that experience—that is, see it in terms of itself. 'I should read all things like braille in this season', she concludes:

> with my fingers I should read them
> lest I go blind in both eyes reading with
> that other eye the final hieroglyph

Although her usual method has been to begin with names, to decode language for what it may reveal about the human condition, MacEwen appears, in *The Shadow-Maker*, to be moving more in the direction of realism. There is one poem, 'The Compass', which is a comic exaggeration of an encounter with a fool who abuses language profoundly on a train between Fredericton and Halifax. Two others, 'Inside the Great Pyramid' and 'One Arab Flute', are reflective accounts of actual experiences and impressions during travel. In terms of poetic technique, MacEwen resembles the incantatory and prophetic Yeats. Yeats claimed to have 'tried to make the language of poetry coincide with that of passionate, normal speech', to have searched for 'a powerful and passionate syntax'. Although she emphasizes the passionate more than the normal aspect of speech, she often combines, like Yeats, the oracular and the vernacular in a single poem. 'O baby, get out of Egypt', she writes in 'Cartaphilus'. 'An ancient slang speaks through me like that.' She employs the dramatic gesture and direct speech ('listen—there was this boy, Manzini') of the actor or storyteller who is intent upon delivering his message. It is a spoken poetry, a poetry of chant or incantation. MacEwen has the habit of reading her own poetry by memory; and the ritual is quite spellbinding. Hers is a passionate plea for life, for beauty. 'To live consciously is holy', she says. The conscious man will not be one-sided; he will find a balance between his passion and his reason, between 'the complex dance of fire and blood' and 'the accurate self'.

Gwendolyn MacEwen was born in Toronto in 1941. She first published poetry when she was fifteen, in the *Canadian Forum*. At eighteen she left school to take up a full-time career as a writer. Her activities and achievements are impressive. Since her Canada Council grant in 1965 to research a historical novel in Egypt, she has received the CBC New Canadian Writing Contest Award (1965), the Borestone Mountain Poetry Award, and the Governor General's Award for *The Shadow-Maker* (1969). She is engaged in translating a modern Arabic novel, preparing plays and talks for radio, and reading poetry in universities and schools.

Her poetry publications include *Selah* (1960) and *The Drunken Clock* (1961) (both privately printed), *The Rising Fire* (1963), *A Breakfast for Barbarians* (1966), and *The Shadow-Maker* (1969). She has published one novel, *Julian the Magician* (1963), and has completed another, *The Twelve Circles of the Night*.

ELI MANDEL

Eli Mandel was born in 1922 in Estevan, Sask., and lived in that province until he joined the Army Medical Corps in 1943 and went overseas. When he returned from the war, he completed an M.A. from the University of Saskatchewan and taught at the Collège Militaire Royale de St Jean. He has since completed a PH.D. in English at the University of Toronto, taught at the University of Alberta, and become a Professor in the Fine Arts and Humanities departments at York University. His first poems were published in *Trio* (1954) with those of Gael Turnbull and Phyllis Webb. He has published three books of poetry: *Fuseli Poems* (1960), *Black and Secret Man* (1964), and *An Idiot Joy* (1967), for which he received the Governor General's Award. Mandel is also an important critic and anthologist; he has an unusual talent for critical synthesis. Apart from his numerous essays, he has published *Criticism: The Silent-Speaking Word*, a series of broadcasts for the CBC. He edited *Poetry '62* (with Jean-Guy Pilon) and *Five Modern Canadian Poets* (1970).

Mandel's early poetry was admired for its use of classical mythology as a means of exploring experience obliquely. His 'Minotaur Poems' and many of the Fuseli poems were written under the critical inspiration of Northrop Frye and the poetic example of James Reaney and Jay Macpherson. The early poems, though they are well-turned, polished pieces, often lack conviction, as if the weight of the traditional masks weakens, or stifles, the poet's own voice. In all of these poems there is a lyrical poet caged and threatening to break out. In *Black and Secret Man* Mandel becomes more personal, more inward. He is, to use his own definition of the modern poet, a man in search of himself; and his voyage of discovery takes him into difficult, troubled waters. He wanders through the ranks of his own ghosts, rifles his personal files of guilt and suffering, discovering in the process new and exciting materials.

The form of Mandel's verse has changed radically. It has moved from a rational ordering of materials in the direction of fragmentation and logical discontinuity, from language that is heavily rhetorical to a more colloquial idiom. Gradually he leaves behind 'the poise and thrust of speech' that 'gleams like polished steel' for a rougher, more halting, though possibly incoherent, form of expression. Some of his latest uncollected poems echo the last speeches of Beckett's characters in combining grunts, non-sequitars, and erratic description with philosophical profundities and lyrical outpourings. Mandel has read and absorbed the critical theories of George Steiner in *Language and Silence*. As a Jew, a writer, and an academic, he is in the natural position to understand the limitations of rational discourse and also the dangers inherent in the indiscriminate use of language. Although his poetic explorations of these themes are sometimes too self-conscious and academic, his new directions are undeniably promising. The Auschwitz poem, for example, is a beautiful rendering of the intellectual and verbal disintegration that accompanies extreme psychic shock, as well as being a profound comment on the labyrinthine nature of moral perception.

Like Atwood, Mandel is fond of perceptual tricks, of unexpected shifts in tone or diction or point of view that startle the reader into consciousness. However, his verse always seems more personal and affective. Atwood, like Flaubert's ideal artist, is everywhere felt but nowhere seen in much of her verse; Mandel, on the other hand, is a poet who is both seen *and* felt. He does not use alienating devices to refine himself out of existence, but to give another dimension to his poetry. It would be foolish to argue that Mandel's materials are more genuinely personal than Atwood's. In a poem such as 'Pictures in an Institution' he claims to reject his Greek and anthropology, his second-hand textbook knowledge, for the raw materials of memory. 'I take,/brutal to my thoughts, these lives, defy/your taste in metaphor', he says. The three self-consciously comic and anti-poetic 'notices' in the poem seem at first designed to cover up the poet's embarrassment at the deeply personal nature of the materials. But that is only one view. It is well to remember that poets are good liars, creatures with a 'forked tongue', to use Mandel's phrase, in which case the 'notices' in the poem could be regarded as devices calculated to *heighten* the personal emphasis by trying to call attention away from it to the banal or the merely comic. That such questions should be raised at all is a fair indication that Mandel is successful in his efforts to create the illusion of fact. Mandel would no doubt agree with Frederick Grove's view that the artist's concern is not with fact but with truth.

For Mandel, the poet is a paradoxical creature, one who partakes of the divine but who also needs to be carefully watched like the wizards, thieves, hunchbacks, and idiots that inhabit his poetic world. The poet, like Houdini, is an escape artist, continually seeking newer and more difficult emotional and verbal nets or mazes to escape from, because he is most alive during those moments of struggle, of challenge. 'I am crazed by poetry,' Mandel admits; but he means the kind of madness that is truly sane, that demands the experience of bondage in order to understand the meaning of liberty. He describes himself as a man 'reeling with messages' and there is in his verse a kind of apocalyptic frenzy, or passionate intensity, that reminds one at times of Layton, at times of Yeats.

JOHN NEWLOVE

There are many dimensions to John Newlove's poetry. To readers familiar with his recent verse the tone of 'wearied intellectuality' that he refers to in 'In This Reed' seems predominant. He writes from a mood of despair and disenchantment that reminds one of tired post-war English poets such as Philip Larkin. Newlove's is a poetry of alienation, peopled with derelicts, hitchhikers, whores, outsiders of all sorts. The poet himself appears as an outsider wandering in some no-man's-land between a vanishing past and a never-to-be-realized future. Memory is another country he inhabits frequently, as he explains in 'The Double-Headed Snake':

> *The greatest*
> *beauty is to be alive, forgetting nothing,*
> *although remembrance hurts*
> *like a foolish act, is a foolish act.*

But memory, like everything else in Newlove's cosmos, breaks down. The vision of *Black Night Window* is dark indeed; but in *The Cave* Newlove's landscape is even more desolate. He moves from the bleakness of the Prairies and the unending highway to a more primal landscape of swamps and sea. It is a book of terse confessions, tortured examinations of failed relationships and breakdowns in communication, cynical meditations upon history and 'progress'. The poet experiences not only the disintegration of personality, of identity, but also the collapse of the objective world; he is a man caught between the engine and the sea; in 'the cave/of time/with trees/ and war/falling/down . . . —and/Jesus,/goodbye,/goodbye.'

In these poems Newlove often writes in a halting, disjunctive, matter-of-fact manner, as in 'Crazy Riel', where he gives the impression of resistance to the poetic process itself. As his vision darkens there is a corresponding paring down of language. The poems become like etchings, painstakingly made, or distillations of complex thoughts and feelings. In *The Cave* Newlove's spareness reaches such a point that he says in 'The Flower': 'I am too tense/decline to dance/verbally.'

There is little reason to expect that Newlove will refine himself out of existence poetically. He has too much talent and has discovered too many new imaginative possibilities. Alongside the poetry of exhaustion and despair are poems of historical interest and poems of great lyrical intensity. He has an exceptional concern for rhythm and cadence and has written short lyrics that rival the best of Cohen and Layton. The pressure to sing, the lyricism, reminds one at times of Dylan Thomas, but without the linguistic inventiveness and excess that characterizes Thomas's poetry. 'Ride Off Any Horizon' best illustrates Newlove's lyricism and his range of poetic materials. It is interesting first of all because it demonstrates one of the primary ways in which Newlove's imagination works. To ride off any horizon is to let the mind follow any idea or feeling for which there is an appropriate sound pattern, to let the mind be carried along by the verbal associations. A similar process is obviously at work in 'Crazy Riel', where the repetition of idea and sound draws attention to the incremental or associational structure of the poem.

The various sections of 'Ride Off Any Horizon' contain almost all of the areas of experience that concern Newlove in his poetry: the vast, untamed Prairies barely touched by the forces of industrialization; the Prairies of the depression; the destruction of the Indians that finds its most powerful expression in 'The Pride', an imaginative recreation of part of our aboriginal heritage; the place of boyhood and family memories and emotional relationships; and, finally, the lonely crowds and concrete wilderness of the city. These images are held together by the refrain both aurally and grammatically, so that the poem has the kind of unity that is usually associated with the narrative or ballad.

Newlove has tried many styles. His imitations of Al Purdy fall flat, as do his attempts to experiment with dialogue and beer-parlour diction. However, he can write with disarming directness and candidness about personal relationships. His is not simply a poetry of self-exposure; he seldom stops short of a precise, rhythmical expression of feeling. Where he cannot find the measure to control a feeling, he will occasionally turn on a gentle but perfectly-pitched irony.

Newlove was born in Regina in 1938 and lived for a number of years in Russian farming communities on the eastern edges of Saskatchewan, where his mother was a school teacher. He has lived and worked in various parts of Canada, in Vancouver, in Terrace, and now in Toronto where he is a senior editor in a publishing company; but the major geographical influence on his life and verse is the Prairies, with its oppressed Indians, ethnic minorities, and the vastness and austerity of its terrain. As he says in *Black Night Window*: 'Everyone is so/lonely in this/country that/it's necessary/to be fantastic.' Newlove's poetry has been widely published in magazines in Canada and abroad and has appeared in numerous anthologies. His publications include *Grave Sirs* (1962), *Elephants, Mothers & Others* (1963), *Moving in Alone* (1965), *Notebook Pages* (1966), *What They Say* (1967), *Black Night Window* (1968), and *The Cave* (1970).

ALDEN NOWLAN

Alden Nowlan has chronicled movingly and convincingly the harshness and hypocrisy of life in the Maritimes. His poems tell of the repressions that are a part of that heritage. 'I am a product', he says 'of a culture that fears any display of emotion and attempts to repress any true communication.' Like Souster, he is moved by his immediate environment, especially by economic conditions that grind down the human spirit. He is a poet of the underprivileged. 'In my childhood and early youth I experienced the kind of poverty that scarifies and warps the soul.' His is a dark world indeed, a world brutalized by poverty, ignorance, fear, greed, and lust. Anyone familiar with the fictional world of Hugh MacLennan's *Each Man's Son* will recognize Nowlan's landscapes at once.

Poetry for Nowlan is a means of establishing communication; like the atheist's prayer, it is a 'reaching out in fear and gentleness'. He is a man who can write of violence, loneliness, and despair with great compassion. In 'Britain Street' he tells of the unhappy conditions between parents and children in the depressed areas, 'where the very names/of their young were curses'. In this climate of brutality and hatred, the poet reclaims the abused, debased names and restores to them some dignity; he gives them a newer, more humane context, invests them with beauty and feeling. He is not a moralist but he is a man capable of fine moral discriminations, as in 'In

Those Old Wars', where he reflects upon the debasing effects of power and the (sometimes) ennobling effects of defeat. His attitude towards his own serious illness is typical:

When I was in hospital, every time that I was operated on I thought I was going to die. The thing I was worried about after worrying about what would become of my wife and son was how much I wanted to write—how much time I'd wasted when I could have been writing. Every time I went down in the elevator to get operated on, I thought . . . how many more things I wanted to say. For that reason, my illness was good for my writing. As Nietzsche says, 'What does not kill me, strengthens me.'

Nowlan claims that his work as a journalist gave him a sense of writing for an audience. 'You learn a great respect for the audience when you do newspaper work,' he says. 'And, another thing, it made me very aware of people.' Not content to be a mere recorder of experience (from the outside), he tries to fathom the psychology that underlies experience, the relation between the feeling and the act. He brings to poetry the novelist's gift of characterization, the capacity to embody a feeling or idea in an image of action. 'I don't like hypocrisy and I don't like fakes,' he says in typical fashion. 'I think the most important division in the world is between the people who are real and the people who are fakes.' Journalism has also left its mark on his style. He writes with a disarming directness and simplicity, as if he had time for neither fakes nor literary games. The pressure to 'get things said' seems to preclude rhetoric, ornament. As he explains in 'And He Wept Aloud':

> oh, admit this, man, there is no point in poetry
> if you withhold the truth
> once you've come by it

The naturalness of Nowlan's diction, his ear for the nuances of the speaking voice, the rightness of his enjambment—these things speak for the sincerity of his desire to offer his truth in the simplest, most unadorned manner possible. As Robert Bly suggests in the prefatory note to *Playing the Jesus Game*, Nowlan is a poet entangled not in words, but in the universe.

Nowlan seems to be a man with few pretensions, personal or literary. Of his own life he says:

Rationally I know that my life is no more important to the cosmos than the life of a housefly or a blade of grass. . . . Emotionally, I can't help but feel that my death will be the end of a world that was created the day I was born.

And of literature? 'Human feeling is all that counts,' he says. 'To hell with literature . . . it's a kind of reassurance that there *are* people out there, listening. Makes me sort of visualize my poems wandering all over the place tapping people on the shoulder and saying: Hi there, I'm Alden Nowlan, who are you?' To the charge that he is a regionalist, Nowlan replies: 'I don't write about Maritime people in capital letters, as if they were some special species. I have certain feelings and responses—I could well have these same feelings and responses if I lived in Montreal, but I'd write about them in a different way, simply because I'd have a different experience and see different things if I lived in Montreal.' Nowlan is no more and no less a regionalist than Faulkner. What needs to be said is that the universal is always best expressed in terms of the concrete, the particular. Nowlan's portrayal of human emotions has moved from the objective early poetry, which was often saved from lapsing into sentimentality by his sense of irony and wry humour, to a more personal, confessional poetry. Whatever his subject or manner, however, his unusual moral sympathy gives the poetry a warmth and an appeal that are irresistible.

Nowlan was born in the Nova Scotia backwoods in 1933. He left school at twelve and worked as a farm labourer, a sawmill helper, the manager of a hillbilly orchestra, and the editor of the Hartland *Observer*, finally joining the *Telegraph-Journal* of St John, N.B. Nowlan has received a number of awards, including Canada Council grants, a Guggenheim fellowship, and a Governor General's Award (for *Bread, Wine and Salt*). He engages in freelance writing projects and is writer-in-residence at the University of New Brunswick. He is married and has one son. His published collections of poetry are *The Rose and the Puritan* (1958), *A Darkness in the Earth* (1959), *Wind in a Rocky Country* (1960), *Under the Ice* (1961), *The Things Which Are* (1962), *Bread, Wine and Salt* (1967), *the mysterious naked man* (1969), and *Playing the Jesus Game* (1970). He has also published drama and short stories, some of which are collected in *Miracle at Indian River* (1968).

MICHAEL ONDAATJE

Michael Ondaatje was born in Ceylon in 1943, where he lived for eleven years. He was educated at Dulwich College in England before coming to Canada in 1962. He studied at Bishop's University, the University of Toronto, and Queen's University, where he completed an M.A. on Edwin Muir. He has published three books of poetry: *The Dainty Monsters* (1967), an exceptionally strong first book; *The Man With Seven Toes* (1969), a macabre narrative set in the primitive wilds of Australia; and *The Collected Works of Billy the Kid* (1970), a novelistic sequence of poems and prose that explores, often in a stream-of-consciousness manner, the physical and psychic life of the famous American folk-hero. Ondaatje is a university lecturer in English. He has published a critical study, *Leonard Cohen* (1970), and is making a film on the poet bp Nichol called *Sons of Captain Poetry*.

Ondaatje has an acute eye for the bizarre, the 'abnormal', the out-of-the-way. His landscapes are peopled with strange beasts, cripples, lost, violent souls, animals—all moving in and out of focus, emerging from and receding into some unchartered region of racial memory. He is fascinated with energy, especially as it is manifested in the form of violence. His poetry is a catalogue of scars, whether the psychic scar that defines an emotional relationship or the disastrous historical event that shapes the destiny of a nation or civilization. Even in the domestic world, which he calls 'a cell of civilized magic', the poet perceives division, the struggle for space and survival.

Thomas Mann remarked that the 'abnormal', the bizarre, is the best, if not the only, route to the 'normal'. Ondaatje's figures, like the parade of freaks and grotesques in a Fellini film, are important for what they reveal of the obsessions, perversions, and fears of so-called normal men. This is not to suggest that his poetry is unrelentingly black or morbid. It is not. He does not revel in the depiction of violence, but brings to bear on his materials considerable integrity and restraint. This is especially obvious in 'Elizabeth' and 'Peter', where the use of understatement heightens the dramatic impact of events. Ondaatje also has a sense of humour, a capacity for the comic and the ironic that is quite engaging. If his characters often have blood on their hands and violence on their minds, they are just as likely to have shaving-cream on their chins and dragons in their tennis nets. His poems never seem to be reworkings of a single feeling or mood, because his ability to assume a variety of points of view enables him to describe events and sensations from the inside, as it were. Furthermore, the strong narrative element keeps him from overloading or overworking a single image and gives the poetry a sense of movement and space.

If Ondaatje has anything that might be called a poetic, it is expressed in his poem ' "The gate in his head": for Victor Coleman'. 'My mind is pouring chaos/in nets onto the page', he writes. Words are the unique threads that, properly woven, can snare strange, unexpected things. Ondaatje recognizes the importance of form in poetry; even his most casual, personal poetry is held together by some linguistic device. But he rejects an undue emphasis on formal structure. In a letter to the editors he states his 'distrust of *all* critics and nearly all dogmatic aesthetics and all rules and all clubs/cliques/ schools of poetry'; instead, he expresses a 'wish to come to each poem and let it breed in its own vacuum and have its own laws and order.' He prefers the 'caught vision' of a blurred photograph to the standard reproduction of a recognizable reality:

> The beautiful formed things caught at the wrong moment
> so they are shapeless, awkward
> moving to the clear.

The wrong moment is the right moment: that is the secret of his peculiar form of myth-making. He catches his subject when it is moving *towards* clarity, when it is neither completely vague and unrecognizable nor completely clear and obvious. He can only use the traditional nets of classical mythology by altering our perception of them, by coming at them from unexpected angles. Otherwise they are too static and destroy the subject they are called upon to illuminate.

Ondaatje says that he has always loved movies and lists his favourites as *The Hustler, Sands of the Kalahari, Once Upon a Time in the West,* and *Point Blank.* Ondaatje's poems have a number of things in common with films: they are intensely *visual*; also, they are frequently *dramatic.* Like the dramatist and film-maker, he is drawn to people and situations and landscapes that are extreme or, at least, uncommon—princesses or escaped convicts, rapes or turning-points in a war, deserts or lush tropical gardens. He is a kind of dramatist of disaster, with a cinematic concern for detail, for the appropriate image, for angles of vision. Like Bergman and Fellini, he has a special talent for finding the striking image, the image that remains hooked in the mind long after other details or events have faded.

AL PURDY

Purdy was born in Wooler, Ont., in 1918 and educated at Albert College in Belleville. At sixteen he dropped out of school and began his wanderings, working at odd jobs, putting in time with the RCAF in British Columbia, and trying his hand at writing. Although his first book of poems was published in 1944, he did not seriously consider supporting himself by writing until he sold a script to the CBC in 1955. He moved to Montreal and then to Roblin Lake at Ameliasburg, where he has lived on and off for the last ten years with the help of his wife, Eurithe, Canada Council grants, and his own ingenuity. From Ameliasburg he has travelled to the Cariboo, Newfoundland, Baffin Island, Cuba, Greece, and England. Of this incessant wandering he says: "I write poems like spiders spin webs, and perhaps for much the same reason, to support my existence . . . unless one is a stone one doesn't sit still. And perhaps new areas of landscape awaken old areas of one's self. One has seen the familiar landscape (perhaps) so often that one ceases to really see it.'

Purdy's development has been haphazard and independent, a product of his continued experiment and chance discovery of interesting talents rather than of absorbing any major influences. He objects as much to the 'sweetness and iambic smoothness' of academic poets like Richard Wilbur as to the 'togetherness . . . of the Duncan-Creeley-Olson bunch.' 'I have no one style,' he said in a letter to Charles Bukowski, 'I have a dozen: have got to be virtuoso enough so I can shift gears like a hot-rod kid—I doubt that my exact combo ever came along before. Unlike some, I have no ideas about being a specific kind of poet. I mean, I don't make rules and say THIS is what a poet HAS to be. I don't know what the hell a poet is or care much. I do know what he isn't sometimes.'

Despite his objections to the contrary, Purdy has developed a speaking voice that is unmistakable. His poetry is most recognizable in terms of its language and structure. One of its main characteristics is a peculiar mixing of chattiness and profundity, of homely observation and mythical or historical allusion. Purdy is an extremely well-read poet. He has a firm grasp of what he calls 'the gear and tackle of living'; the imagery in a single poem can be drawn from a number of different sources, sometimes with considerable success. He peoples his rural Ontario with ghosts from the near and distant past, with echoes of ancient Greece and United Empire Loyalist salons; in his particular Baffin Island may be seen the shades of Diefenbaker, Odysseus, Laurence Olivier, King John, and Gary Cooper.

Structurally, Purdy's verse is equally recognizable. He has a tendency to leave his poems open-ended, to leave a subject deliberately unresolved. In poems of this sort there is no subject outside the poem other than the perceiving consciousness of the poet; in other words, the subject of the poem is *the process itself*, the process of trying to come to terms with a feeling or experience. Philosophically, a preoccupation with process is understandable; it implies an awareness that at best 'truth' is difficult to discover, at worst it is completely relative. From an aesthetic point of view, however, a desire for honesty and verisimilitude in this area does not always work to the poem's advantage. Carried too far it can become a cliché, a short-cut. If this happens the reader is likely to feel that at times a poet should lie, that he should be prepared to offer up small truths directly rather than try unsuccessfully for the larger truth.

Whatever objections one may have to Purdy's open-endedness and his habit of undercutting something that is obviously important to both himself and the reader, there can be no doubt about his very considerable talent. His 'exact combo' *is* unlike anything else in Canadian poetry. He has an inexhaustible capacity to surprise and delight, to upset whatever critical expectations his own poems might encourage. His answer to his critics, and perhaps the reason for his popularity, is suggested in the following comment he makes on the nature of the poetic process:

> *There ought to be a quality in a good poet beyond any analysis, the part of his mind that leaps from one point to another, sideways, backwards, ass-over-electric-kettle. This quality is not logic, and the result may not be consistent with the rest of the poem when it happens, though it may be. I believe it is said by medicos that much of the human mind has no known function. Perhaps the leap sideways and backwards comes from there. At any rate, it seems to me the demands made on it cause the mind to stretch, to do more than it is capable of under ordinary and different circumstances. And when this happens, or when you think it does, that time is joyous, and you experience something beyond experience. Like discovering you can fly, or that relative truth may blossom into an absolute. And the absolute must be attacked again and again, until you find something that will stand up, may not be denied, which becomes a compass point by which to move somewhere else. . . . And sometimes—if you're lucky—a coloured fragment may slip through into the light when you're writing a poem.*

There are many coloured fragments in Purdy's poetry. The way his mind stretches to assimilate new areas of experience, the way it leaps in unexpected directions, often at considerable psychic cost to the poet, is truly remarkable.

Purdy's best verse is predominantly elegaic. Like Roberts and Carman, he is sensitive to manifestations of change, to the passing of time. He loves to reflect upon things historical. There is something about events and people out of the past that releases his imagination in new and exciting ways. Thus his identification with the decaying world of Prince Edward County, his attraction to the outbacks of British Columbia, and his passionate response to the Eskimo's encounter with the white man's technology on Baffin Island. Perhaps the values, the certainty, that the shifting present never affords him are found in abundance in the past. In poems such as 'The Runners' and 'Lament for the Dorsets' there is little uncertainty or self-consciousness; instead, the poet achieves a rare beauty and precision.

Since the publication of his first book in 1944, Purdy has published a number of major collections, including *Poems for All the Annettes* (1962, 1968), *The Cariboo Horses* (1965), for which he received the Governor General's Award, *North of Summer* (1967), *Wild Grape Wine* (1968), and *Love in a Burning Building* (1970). He has also published a limited deluxe edition of poems from his trip to Greece called *The Quest for Ouzo* (1970). In addition, Purdy has edited an anthology of poems for schools, *Fifteen Winds*, and a collection of Canadian views of the United States, *The New Romans*.

RAYMOND SOUSTER

Souster's chief concern has been to keep singing in the face of despair. As he says in 'Good Fortune', 'life isn't a matter of luck/of good fortune, it's whether/the heart can keep singing/when there's really no reason/why it should.' His imagination is peopled with the victims of wars and industrial 'progress', whores, cripples, beggars, down-and-outs of every sort. He takes upon himself their guilt and shame and tries to communicate the terrible sense of human waste that weighs upon him. Souster is equally troubled by the impermanence of things. At times he displays a gentle nostalgia for the innocence and good times of the past, lamenting the passing of friends and shared interests and the disappearance of familiar landscapes under a jungle of concrete and cereal-box architecture. Although he is incapable of sustained irony or satire, Souster often strikes out at the instruments of change and destruction like an animal that has been hurt or cornered. His most convincing response is to celebrate signs of man's capacity for joy or, at least, survival; he searches out pockets of beauty and spontaneity in the rubbish-heap of the century, as in 'Top Hat' or 'Victory', where he celebrates the determination of a 'bum' who beats the street-cleaning machine to a castaway cigarette butt.

Souster is predominantly a poet of content. Robert Creeley applies this name to the poets of the thirties. 'There are also those men', he says,' . . . who extend to their writing of verse concerns which haunt them, again reasonably enough, in other areas of living. They are in this way poets of "content", and their poems argue images of living to which the content of their poem points. They argue the poem as a means to recognition, a signboard as it were, not in itself a structure of "recognition" or—better—cognition itself.' Creeley is thinking here of Kenneth Fearing, but his description applies well to Souster, for whom the sociological impulse seems more pressing than the aesthetic. This view is not inconsistent with Souster's idea of the poet's function. In 'The Lilac Poem' he speaks of the impermanence of all things, even poetry. If art itself is subject to the eroding effects of time, the artist is best employed as a recorder or photographer of the human condition at a particular moment in history; or rather—and perhaps this is his main function— as an entertainer who can divert man's attention away from the sources of his despair. The short poem is itself a function of the poet's view of the impermanence of all things; and it is especially characteristic of modern poetry. As Frost suggests, the good poem provides 'a momentary stay against confusion.'

This does not mean that Souster has no interest in form, in prosody. He is sufficiently steeped in American poetry, especially in the work of Ezra Pound and William Carlos Williams, to have absorbed not only a distaste for the baggage of poetic tradition, but also a preoccupation with certain formal elements in verse. His own poetry is not metrical; he prefers the shifting rhythms of speech to the monotony of the metronome. Like Bowering, he avoids the use of mythical allusion and archaism, preferring instead poetry with a base in actual experience. Souster understands Pound's dictum that 'It is better to present one Image in a lifetime than to produce voluminous works.' He has written a number of excellent imagist poems, such as 'Study: The Bath' and 'The Six-Quart Basket', that have the clarity and economy of the *haiku*. Occasionally Souster is tempted to comment on the image, to tag on a moral that leaves attention outside the poem, as in 'The Hunter'; but his best poems are either pure image or pure voice. The poems of lyrical reflection are less likely to misfire, because the poet begins with a mood that is strong enough to arrange the materials it gathers to express itself, rather than with an image that is often too weak to support itself without assistance from the voice of the poet. These reflective verses speak for Souster's integrity as a man and as a poet; they are beautifully turned and reveal a quiet concern, or empathy, that is always surprising, sometimes moving.

Souster was born in Toronto in 1921 and has spent all of his life there except for the war years, 1941-5, when he was in the RCAF in the Maritimes and in England. Of his beloved Toronto, he says:

I suppose I am truly an unrepentant regionalist. As Emile Zola put it to Paul Bourget: 'Why should we be everlastingly wanting to escape to lands of romance? Our streets are full of tragedy and full of beauty; they should be enough for any poet.' All the experiences one is likely to encounter in Paris can be found in this city. Toronto has a flavour all its own.... My roots are here; this is the place that tugs at my heart when I leave it and fills me with quiet relief when I return to it.

Like Wallace Stevens, Souster is wedded simultaneously to the muses of poetry and commerce: as well as being a serious poet, he has been employed for many years by the Canadian Imperial Bank of Commerce in downtown Toronto. His involvements in the poetic community are many. He edited a mimeographed magazine called *Combustion* (1957-60) and was a founder-editor of Contact Press. He edited *New Wave Canada: The New Explosion in Canadian Poetry* (1966), and *Generation Now* (1970), an anthology of poetry for schools.

Souster has published more than a dozen books of poetry, including *When We Are Young* (1946), *Go to Sleep, World* (1947), *Shake Hands With the Hangman* (1953), *Selected Poems* (1956), edited by Louis Dudek, *A Local Pride* (1962), *Place of Meeting* (1962), *The Colour of the Times* (1964), his collected poems, which received the Governor General's Award, *Ten Elephants on Yonge Street* (1965), *As Is* (1967), *Lost & Found* (1968), and *So Far So Good* (1969).

SUPPLEMENTARY MATERIALS

1. Criticism: General

Dudek, Louis, and Michael Gnarowski, eds. *The Making of Modern Poetry in Canada* (Toronto, 1967).

Jones, D.G. *Butterfly on Rock* (Toronto, 1970).

———— 'The Sleeping Giant; Or the Uncreated Conscience of the Race', *Canadian Literature*, 26 (Autumn 1965). Reprinted in *A Choice of Critics*, ed. George Woodcock (Toronto, 1966).

Klinck, Carl F., ed. *Literary History of Canada: Canadian Literature in English* (Toronto, 1965).

Mandel, Eli. 'A Lack of Ghosts: Canadian Poets and Poetry', *The Humanities Association Bulletin*, XVI, 1 (Spring 1965).

———— 'Modern Canadian Poetry', *Twentieth Century Literature*, XVI, 3 (July 1970).

Reaney, James. 'The Canadian Poet's Predicament', *University of Toronto Quarterly* XXVI, 3 (April 1957).

Smith, A.J.M. 'The Canadian Poet: Part I. To Confederation; Part II. After Confederation', *Canadian Literature*, 37 & 38 (Summer & Autumn 1968).

———— 'Eclectic Detachment: Aspects of Identity in Canadian Poetry', *Canadian Literature*, 9 (Summer 1961). Reprinted in *A Choice of Critics*, ed. George Woodcook (Toronto, 1966).

———— 'Introduction', *The Oxford Book of Canadian Verse*, ed. A.J.M. Smith (Toronto, 1960).

————, ed. *Masks of Poetry* (Toronto, 1962).

Waddington, Miriam. 'Canadian Tradition and Canadian Literature', *Journal of Commonwealth Literature*, 8 (December 1969).

Wilson, Milton. 'Other Canadians and After', *The Tamarack Review*, 9 (Autumn 1958). Reprinted in *The First Five Years*, ed. Robert Weaver (Toronto, 1962).

Woodcock, George, ed. *A Choice of Critics: Selections from 'Canadian Literature'* (Toronto, 1966).

2. Criticism: Individual

MARGARET ATWOOD

Marshall, Tom. 'Les animaux de son pays: Notes sur la poésie de Margaret Atwood', *Ellipse*, 3 (Spring 1970).

MARGARET AVISON

Ghiselin, Brewster. 'The Architecture of Vision', *Poetry*, LXX, 6 (September 1947).

Jones, Lawrence M. 'A Core of Brilliance: Margaret Avison's Achievement', *Canadian Literature*, 38 (Autumn 1968).

Redekop, Ernest. *Margaret Avison* (Toronto, 1970).

Wilson, Milton. 'The Poetry of Margaret Avison', *Canadian Literature*, 2 (Autumn 1959). Reprinted in *A Choice of Critics*, ed. George Woodcock (Toronto, 1966).

EARLE BIRNEY

Smith, A.J.M. 'A Unified Personality: Birney's Poems', *Canadian Literature*, 30 (Autumn 1966).

West, Paul. 'Earle Birney and the Compound Ghost', *Canadian Literature*, 13 (Summer 1962). Reprinted in *A Choice of Critics*, ed. George Woodcock (Toronto, 1966).

Wilson, Milton. 'Poet Without a Muse', *Canadian Literature*, 30 (Autumn 1966).

LEONARD COHEN

Davey, Frank. 'Leonard Cohen and Bob Dylan: Poetry and the Popular Song', *Alphabet*, 17 (December 1969).

Djwa, Sandra. 'Leonard Cohen: Black Romantic', *Canadian Literature*, 34 (Autumn 1967).

Ondaatje, Michael. *Leonard Cohen* (Toronto, 1970).

Pacey, Desmond. 'The Phenomenon of Leonard Cohen', *Canadian Literature*, 34 (Autumn 1967).

Purdy, A.W. 'Leonard Cohen: A Personal Look', *Canadian Literature*, 23 (Winter 1965).

IRVING LAYTON

Mandel, Eli. *Irving Layton* (Toronto, 1969).

Woodcock, George. 'A Grab at Proteus: Notes on Irving Layton', *Canadian Literature*, 28 (Spring 1966).

GWENDOLYN MACEWEN

Atwood, Margaret. 'MacEwen's Muse', *Canadian Literature*, 45 (Summer 1970).

ELI MANDEL

Ower, John. 'Black and Secret Poet: Notes on Eli Mandel', *Canadian Literature*, 42 (Autumn 1969).

ALDEN NOWLAN

Cook, Gregory. 'An *Amethyst* Extra: Interview with Alden Nowlan', *Amethyst*, II, 4 (Summer 1963).

The Fiddlehead, 81 (August, September, October 1969). Special issue devoted to Alden Nowlan.

MICHAEL ONDAATJE

Kahn, Sy. 'Michael Ondaatje, *The Dainty Monsters*', *The Far Point*, 1 (Fall/Winter 1968).

AL PURDY

Bowering, George. *Al Purdy* (Toronto, 1970).

Geddes, Gary. 'A.W. Purdy: An Interview', *Canadian Literature*, 41 (Summer 1969). Reprinted in *20th-Century Poetry & Poetics*, ed. Gary Geddes (Toronto, 1969).

Stevens, Peter. 'In the Raw: The Poetry of A.W. Purdy', *Canadian Literature*, 28 (Spring 1966).

RAYMOND SOUSTER

Carruth, Hayden. 'To Souster from Vermont', *Tamarack Review*, 34 (Winter 1965).

Dudek, Louis. 'Groundhog Among the Stars: The Poetry of Raymond Souster', *Canadian Literature*, 22 (Autumn 1964). Reprinted in *A Choice of Critics*, ed. George Woodcock (Toronto, 1966).

3. Audio-Visual Aids

RECORDS

Canadian Poets I. Eight poets, including Birney, Bowering, Cohen, Layton, MacEwen, Newlove, and

Purdy, reading selections from their own works on two 12-inch LPs. CBC publications, $7.50

Canadian Poets II: The Journals of Susanna Moodie by Margaret Atwood. Read by Mia Anderson. CBC publications, $5.00

Six Montreal Poets. Includes Cohen and Layton. Folkways 9805

Six Toronto Poets. Includes Avison and Souster. Folkways 9806

Songs from a Room by Leonard Cohen. Columbia 9767

Songs of Leonard Cohen. Columbia 2733

FILMS

Ladies and Gentlemen, Mr Leonard Cohen. National Film Board. 44 min.

A Moving Feast. Includes Birney, Layton, MacEwen. May be rented from Metropolitan Educational Television Association (META), 31 Wellesley St E., Toronto 284. 18 min., 40 sec.

TAPES

Canadian Poets on Tape. Nine audio tapes available from Publications Department, Ontario Institute for Studies in Education, 252 Bloor St W., Toronto 5. Included are Birney, Layton, MacEwen, Mandel, Purdy, and Souster. 30 min., $5.00 each

High Barnet cassette tapes. Ten poetry tapes available, including Atwood, Birney, Layton, MacEwen, Mandel, Purdy, and Souster. High Barnet, 503 Merton St, Toronto 7. 1 hr, $12.95 each

Irving Layton. 2-inch video. May be rented from Metropolitan Educational Television Association (META), 31 Wellesley St E., Toronto 284. 28 min., 45 sec.

Irving Layton: Under Attack. Explains the role of the poet and defends Canadian poetry. Audio tape may be obtained from Traffic Department, Screen Gems, 72 Carlton St, Toronto 200. $10.00-$15.00

Portrait of a Canadian Poet — Earle Birney. Talks to students about poetry and recent social issues. 2-inch video. May be rented from META. 28 min., 32 sec.

INDEX

Four Strong Winds

- fall - coming of bad times
- summer - good time
- ~~winter~~ - bad
  winter
- metaphor of the road
- summer of love affair
- colloquial

Waiter There Is An Alligator In
My Coffee

- satire on cheap lines
- most outrageous things happen & no one
  gets excited.

The Execution

- grisley humor
- case of mistaken identity
- reporter comes to cover hanging - & is mistaken
- waiting for coroner - tense - mistaken
  "   "   priest   "
  "   "   Mr. Ellis - criminal

- whole thing ends on an illogical note - if they
  killed him he wouldn't be telling it.